Pick Your Stitch, Build a Blanket

80 Knit Stitches, Endless Combinations

Doreen L. Marquart

Martingale®
Create with Confidence

Dedication

To my husband, Gordon.

Thank you for all the encouragement and support you give me.
I would never have been able to accomplish what I have without
your willingness to pitch in and help wherever needed!

Pick Your Stitch, Build a Blanket:
80 Knit Stitches, Endless Combinations
© 2015 by Doreen L. Marquart

Martingale®
19021 120th Ave. NE, Ste. 102
Bothell, WA 98011-9511 USA
ShopMartingale.com

Printed in China
20 19 18 17 16 15   8 7 6 5 4 3 2 1

Library of Congress Cataloging-in-Publication Data
is available upon request.

ISBN: 978-1-60468-448-3

Mission Statement

Dedicated to providing quality products and
service to inspire creativity.

Credits

PUBLISHER AND CHIEF VISIONARY OFFICER: Jennifer Erbe Keltner
EDITOR IN CHIEF: Mary V. Green
DESIGN DIRECTOR: Paula Schlosser
MANAGING EDITOR: Karen Costello Soltys
ACQUISITIONS EDITOR: Karen M. Burns
TECHNICAL EDITOR: Donna Druchunas
COPY EDITOR: Marcy Heffernan
PRODUCTION MANAGER: Regina Girard
COVER AND INTERIOR DESIGNER: Connor Chin
PHOTOGRAPHER: Brent Kane
ILLUSTRATOR: Connor Chin

Acknowledgments

I would like to thank:

My good friends Karen Kuckenbecker, Barbara
Ockleman, and Ingrid Stroh, for sharing your
thoughts, ideas, and suggestions throughout
the entire process of creating this book. I am so
thankful for your friendship and continued support.

Bailey Alexander, for knitting many of the sample
blocks, for listening to me when I was frustrated
that the designs in my head wouldn't jump readily
onto the paper, and for working extra hours in the
shop so I could devote the time necessary to bring
this project to life.

Thank you to all the fantastic yarn companies
I have the pleasure to work with: Berroco, Cascade
Yarns, Claudia Hand Painted Yarns, Frog Tree Yarns,
Hikoo, Jojoland, Malabrigo Yarn, and Westminster
Fibers, Inc.

And to Martingale, for once again having
confidence and faith in me and enthusiasm equal
to mine in making this book a reality!

Contents

Bonus project online!

    Visit www.ShopMartingale.com/extras to download "Foaming Waves Afghan" for free.

Introduction

As the owner of a yarn shop, I often recommend *365 Knitting Stitches a Year Perpetual Calendar* (Martingale, 2002) to my customers. Not only is it a great calendar that can be used year after year, but it's also a wonderful source of inspiration. I've turned to this calendar many times for different stitch ideas for afghans.

One thing I've found, however, is that a vast number of knitters don't know how to adapt and use these stitch patterns to actually knit an afghan. Some want to simply use a single pattern to make a baby blanket, lap robe, or full-sized afghan, but aren't sure how to figure out how many stitches to cast on. Others would like to make a multiple-block afghan, but aren't sure which patterns to combine or how to make sure all the blocks will turn out the same size so they can be easily assembled into a blanket.

That's where this book will help you. I've completed the necessary calculations for 80 of the stitch patterns from the calendar so that no matter what yarn or needle size you use, as long as you use the *same* yarn weight and needle size for each block, your finished blocks will be identical in size, after blocking. I've also included a section on how to do the necessary math so that you're not limited to the stitch patterns included here but can use any single stitch pattern to make any size afghan you desire.

Once you discover how easy the entire process is, a whole new world of possible uses for the calendar will be at your fingertips. Let the fun begin!

Getting Started

The size block you end up with totally depends on the yarn and needles you choose to use. Using a fingering-weight yarn and needles appropriate for that weight yarn will yield a smaller block than if you were to use a worsted- or bulky-weight yarn. It's important to spend time checking your gauge and doing a little bit of planning before you dive in and start knitting an afghan.

Gauge

Knitters often feel that making a gauge swatch isn't important, especially if what they're knitting isn't a garment and doesn't have to fit anyone. However, even with blankets and afghans, you'll want to know what size your project will turn out to be. And with multiple-block afghans, you'll want to make sure all your blocks are the same size for easy assembly. The photo below shows how much of a difference the yarn weight/needle size—and thus "gauge"—can make. All samples were knit with the same number of stitches and the same number of rows.

The good news is, in the stitch-pattern directions that start on page 10, all the math has been done. So as long as you use the same size needle and yarn for each block, the blocks will be the same size after blocking. Select the yarn weight you wish to use and needles in the size appropriate for that yarn, and let's get started with one of the most important steps—testing your gauge.

Start by making the Stockinette Stitch block (page 11). By beginning here, you'll not only be able to determine your gauge, but you'll also be completing the first block for your afghan. Even if you don't plan to use a "plain" block in your finished afghan, take the time to knit this block first. From this block you will be able to determine the finished size of each and every other block you make, and thus calculate how many blocks you'll need to knit for the size afghan you want to make.

Decide if you want to make the smaller or larger blocks (instructions for each stitch pattern include two sizes), then cast on accordingly and knit the Stockinette Stitch block.

Lay the completed block flat on the table and measure its size. It's actually best if you block it first, being careful not to stretch it. This block will act as a gauge and size guideline for every other block.

Refer to the table below to see the width your block will be, based on the gauge. (The length will be determined by the number of rows you knit.) While I normally prefer to work in fractions, this table uses decimals so you can get a very precise comparison of what the exact finished sizes of the blocks would be with just a slight difference in the gauge.

Block Size Based on Gauge

Your Gauge	30-Stitch Block	46-Stitch Block
3.5 sts/inch	8.57"	13.14"
3.75 sts/inch	8.00"	12.27"
4.0 sts/inch	7.50"	11.50"
4.25 sts/inch	7.06"	10.82"
4.5 sts/inch	6.67"	10.22"
4.75 sts/inch	6.32"	9.68"
5.0 sts/inch	6.00"	9.20"
5.25 sts/inch	5.71"	8.76"
5.50 sts/inch	5.45"	8.36"
5.75 sts/inch	5.22"	8.00"
6.00 sts/inch	5.00"	7.67"

As you can see by reviewing the chart, the more stitches per inch you have, the smaller the finished block will be. Likewise, the smaller the finished block, the more individual blocks you will have to make for a finished afghan.

How Many Blocks Do I Need?

Once you've determined your gauge, then you can figure out how many blocks you need to knit to make the size afghan you want. What size afghan do you want to make? I use the following as a guideline for the sizes of my afghans.

Size	Width x Length
Carriage size	24" x 30"
Crib/baby-blanket size	30" x 36"
Lap robe	36" x 45"
Full-sized afghan	45" x 54"

Keep in mind that these sizes are just guidelines, and you don't have to use these *exact* numbers. You just want your finished size to be somewhere around those numbers. My own "rule" is that I want the length of my finished afghan to be approximately 4" to 8" longer than the width. For example, if I'm making a baby blanket that's 32" wide, I'll make the length approximately 36". If my lap robe is 36" wide, then I'd strive for the length to be about 44". For a full-sized afghan, if the width is 46", then I'd aim for 54" in length.

Let's say you decide you're going to make the 30-stitch blocks using worsted-weight yarn, and you've determined your gauge is 5 stitches per inch. This means that the width of your block will be approximately 6" (30 ÷ 5 = 6, or number of stitches divided by gauge equals the finished width).

Once you've knit and measured your Stockinette Stitch block, you can determine how many blocks you'll need for the size afghan you want to make.

In the blocks I made as samples, my finished measurements using worsted-weight yarn were 6" wide x 7.25" long. (That's right, they aren't square, but rather rectangular.) Therefore, I could use the following number of blocks for each respective size blanket.

- **Carriage size:** 5 blocks x 5 blocks = 30" x 36.25" (25 blocks total)
- **Crib/baby-blanket size:** 6 blocks x 6 blocks = 36" x 43.50" (36 blocks total)
- **Lap robe:** 7 blocks x 7 blocks = 42" x 50.75" (49 blocks total)
- **Full-sized afghan:** 8 blocks x 8 blocks = 48" x 58" (64 blocks total)

Naturally you don't have to make your afghan the same number of blocks wide as you do long. Using the finished size of your Stockinette Stitch block, you can calculate the number of squares that will be needed for the afghan length you desire.

How Much Yarn Do I Need?

Below are guidelines to help you decide how much yarn you'll need for different-size afghans made from each of the different yarn weights. This table is intended to give you a starting point. The more involved the pattern stitches are, the more yarn you will need. For example, if you choose many of the cable patterns rather than simpler stitches like the Fleck or Waffle stitch, you may need to allow for an extra skein or two of yarn. Since a reputable yarn shop will take back any extra skeins of yarn (providing they are still in saleable condition, of course), it's always a good idea to purchase more than you think you are going to need—just in case.

Block Borders

All of the individual patterns have been written as finished blocks complete with a garter-stitch border. You could choose to use seed stitch, moss stitch, or any other edging that doesn't curl instead of garter stitch. However, you'll want to use some type of border so that the blocks don't curl under on the sides and you have nice edges to use for seaming them all together.

Yardage Required by Yarn Weight and Project Size

Afghan Size	Fingering	Sport/DK	Worsted	Bulky
Carriage size: 24" x 30"	1250	1075	830	560
Crib/baby-blanket Size: 30" x 36"	1850	1600	1240	870
Lap robe: 36" x 45"	2800	2400	2000	1550
Full-sized afghan: 45" x 54"	4200	3600	2800	1950

Single-Pattern Projects

Any of the 80 stitch patterns contained in this book would be lovely by itself in an afghan.

The main thing you have to do after choosing a stitch pattern is to determine how many stitches to cast on in order to end up with the size afghan you desire. Again, I suggest making up the Stockinette Stitch block (page 11) to get an accurate stitch gauge. From this sample, you can easily figure out how many stitches you need to cast on for your afghan.

Multiples

Let's say you want to make an afghan that measures 40" wide.

Calculations	For Example	Your Numbers
Desired finished width	40"	_____
Multiply by number of stitches per inch	x 5 stitches per inch	× _____
Total number of stitches to cast on	= cast on 200 stitches	= _____
Total number of stitches needed to attain desired width	200 stitches	_____
Subtract stitches required for border (remember to subtract for both sides)	− 10 stitches (5 stitches from each side)	− _____
Number of pattern stitches required	= 190 pattern stitches	= _____

Now you have to take into account the stitch repeat. Notice that at the top of each stitch pattern, the multiple of that stitch pattern is given. This is extremely important information, information that you'll want to pay close attention to when figuring out how many stitches to cast on.

Pick out the pattern stitch you wish to use. For this example, I used a stitch with a multiple of 4 sts + 1 st.

Calculations	For Example	Your Numbers
Number of pattern stitches	190 stitches	_____
Subtract extra stitches needed to complete pattern repeat	− 1 (multiple of 4 stitches +1 stitch)	− _____
Divide by number of stitches in each pattern repeat	÷ 4 stitches per repeat	÷ _____
Equals the number of times pattern will be repeated	= 47¼	= _____
The number of pattern repeats *must* be a whole number. If necessary, add or subtract a few stitches in order for this to be a whole number.	47 × 4 = 188 pattern stitches; or 48 × 4 = 192 pattern stitches. Work either 47 or 48 repeats.	= _____

Borders

For most stitch patterns, you can simply cast on the number of stitches you need for the desired width of your afghan and not be concerned about the transition from the border to the pattern stitch. However, there are a few exceptions.

When making a cabled afghan, such as the Triple Cable Afghan (page 78), you'll need to increase after the bottom border is completed. Cables tend to draw the knitted fabric together; if you don't increase the number of stitches, you'll find that the border will ruffle and be unattractive. Generally, increase one stitch for every four stitches used in the cable. Thus if you're knitting an eight-stitch cable and are working nine cables across the width of your afghan, increase 18 stitches across the first row of your pattern. Make sure to increase in the actual pattern section of your afghan and not over the side-border stitches. Remember to decrease the same number of stitches when you work the first row of the top border.

Likewise, if you're knitting a lace pattern, you'll want to decrease some stitches.

The Blocks

This section contains 80 different stitch patterns. All of them have been adapted (by either adding or subtracting stitches) so that no matter which type of yarn you use, as long as you use the *same* yarn and *same* needle size for each stitch pattern, the result will be blocks that are the same size. Refer to this section for the various stitch patterns used throughout the book. When you make any of the projects, you can substitute stitch patterns if you desire. Instructions are given for making either a small or large block in each pattern stitch.

- Small blocks have 30 cast-on stitches and are worked for 48 rows.

- Large blocks have 46 cast-on stitches and are worked for 80 rows.

- Both sizes are worked with garter-stitch borders on all four sides of the block.

Stockinette Stitch

Stitch Pattern

Any number of sts

Row 1 (RS): Knit.

Row 2: Purl.

Rep these 2 rows for patt.

Making a Block

To make Small (Large) block with border:

CO 30 (46) sts.

Knit 6 (10) rows.

Keeping first and last 3 (5) sts in garter st, work rows 1 and 2 of Stockinette Stitch patt over rem sts.

Rep rows 1 and 2 another 17 (29) times for a total of 36 (60) patt rows.

Knit 6 (10) rows.

BO kw on RS.

Garter-Stitch Ridges

Stitch Pattern

Any number of sts

Row 1 (RS): Knit.

Row 2: Purl.

Row 3: Knit.

Row 4: Purl.

Rows 5–10: Purl.

Rep these 10 rows for patt.

Making a Block

To make Small (Large) block with border:

CO 30 (46) sts.

Knit 6 (10) rows.

Keeping first and last 3 (5) sts in garter stitch, work rows 1–10 of Garter-Stitch Ridges patt over rem sts. Rep rows 1–10 another 2 (5) times and then work rows 1–6 another 1 (0) time for a total of 36 (60) patt rows.

Knit 6 (10) rows.

BO kw on RS.

Diagonal Seed Stitch

Stitch Pattern

Multiple of 6 sts

Row 1 (RS): *K5, P1; rep from * to end.

Row 2: P1, *K1, P5; rep from * to last 5 sts, K1, P4.

Row 3: K3, *P1, K5; rep from * to last 3 sts, P1, K2.

Row 4: P3, *K1, P5; rep from * to last 3 sts, K1, P2.

Row 5: K1, *P1, K5; rep from * to last 5 sts, P1, K4.

Row 6: *P5, K1; rep from * to end.

Rep these 6 rows for patt.

Making a Block

To make Small (Large) block with border:

CO 30 (46) sts.

Knit 6 (10) rows.

Keeping first and last 3 (5) sts in garter st, work rows 1–6 of Diagonal Seed Stitch patt over rem sts. Rep rows 1–6 another 5 (9) times for a total of 36 (60) patt rows.

Knit 6 (10) rows.

BO kw on RS.

Horizontal Two-One Ribs

Stitch Pattern

Multiple of 3 sts + 1 st

Rows 1 and 3 (RS): Knit.

Rows 2 and 4: Purl.

Row 5: K1, *P2, K1; rep from * to end.

Row 6: *K1, P2; rep from * to last st, K1.

Row 7: P1, *K2, P1; rep from * to end.

Rows 8 and 10: Purl.

Rows 9 and 11: Knit.

Row 12: Purl.

Rep these 12 rows for patt.

Making a Block

To make Small (Large) block with border:

CO 30 (46) sts.

Knit 5 (9) rows.

Dec row: K8 (14), K2tog, K10 (14), K2tog, K8 (14)—28 (44) sts.

Keeping first and last 3 (5) sts in garter st, work rows 1–12 of Horizontal Two-One Ribs patt over rem sts. Rep rows 1–12 another 2 (4) times for a total of 36 (60) patt rows.

Inc row: K7 (13), M1, K14 (18), M1, K7 (13)—30 (46) sts.

Knit 5 (9) rows.

BO kw on RS.

Piqué Check Stitch

Stitch Pattern

Multiple of 6 sts

Rows 1, 3, and 5 (RS): Knit.

Row 2 and all even-numbered rows: Purl.

Rows 7, 9, and 11: *K3, P3; rep from * to end.

Rows 13, 15, and 17: Knit.

Rows 19, 21, and 23: *P3, K3; rep from * to end.

Row 24: Purl.

Rep these 24 rows for patt.

Making a Block

To make Small (Large) block with border:

CO 30 (46) sts.

Knit 6 (10) rows.

Keeping first and last 3 (5) sts in garter st, work rows 1–24 of Piqué Check Stitch patt over rem sts.

Rep rows 1–12 (1–24) once more and then work rows 1–12 another 0 (1) times for a total of 36 (60) patt rows.

Knit 6 (10) rows.

BO kw on RS.

Fleck Stitch

Stitch Pattern

Multiple of 2 sts + 1 st

Row 1 (RS): Knit.

Row 2: Purl.

Row 3: K1, *P1, K1; rep from * to end.

Row 4: Purl.

Rep these 4 rows for patt.

Making a Block

To make Small (Large) block with border:

CO 30 (46) sts.

Knit 5 (9) rows.

Inc row: K15 (23), M1, K15 (23)—31 (47) sts.

Keeping first and last 3 (5) sts in garter st, work rows 1–4 of Fleck Stitch patt over rem sts.

Rep rows 1–4 another 8 (14) times for a total of 36 (60) patt rows.

Dec row: K15 (23), K2tog, K14 (22)—30 (46) sts.

Knit 5 (9) rows.

BO kw on RS.

Check Pattern

Stitch Pattern

Multiple of 3 sts + 1 st

Row 1 (RS): Knit.

Row 2: Purl.

Row 3: K1, *P2, K1; rep from * to end.

Row 4: Purl.

Rep these 4 rows for patt.

Making a Block

To make Small (Large) block with border:

CO 30 (46) sts.

Knit 5 (9) rows.

Inc row: K15 (23), M1, K15 (23)—31 (47) sts.

Keeping first and last 3 (5) sts in garter st, work rows 1–4 of Check Pattern over rem sts. Rep rows 1–4 another 8 (14) times for a total of 36 (60) patt rows.

Dec row: K15 (23), K2tog, K14 (22)—30 (46) sts.

Knit 5 (9) rows.

BO kw on RS.

Waffle Stitch

Stitch Pattern

Multiple of 3 sts + 1 st

Rows 1 and 3 (RS): P1, *K2, P1; rep from * to end.

Row 2: K1, *P2, K1; rep from * to end.

Row 4: Knit.

Rep these 4 rows for patt.

Making a Block

To make Small (Large) block with border:

CO 30 (46) sts.

Knit 5 (9) rows.

Inc row: K15 (23), M1, K15 (23)—31 (47) sts.

Keeping first and last 3 (5) sts in garter st, work rows 1–4 of Waffle Stitch patt over rem sts.

Rep rows 1–4 another 8 (14) times for a total of 36 (60) patt rows.

Dec row: K15 (23), K2tog, K14 (22)—30 (46) sts.

Knit 5 (9) rows.

BO kw on RS.

Purled Ladder Stitch

Stitch Pattern

Multiple of 4 sts + 2 sts

Rows 1 and 2: Knit.

Row 3 (RS): P2, *K2, P2; rep from * to end.

Row 4: K2, *P2, K2; rep from * to end.

Rows 5 and 6: Knit.

Row 7: Rep row 4.

Row 8: P2, *K2, P2; rep from * to end.

Rep these 8 rows for patt.

Making a Block

To make Small (Large) block with border:

CO 30 (46) sts.

Knit 5 (9) rows.

Dec row: K8 (14), K2tog, K10 (14), K2tog, K8 (14)—28 (44) sts.

Keeping first and last 3 (5) sts in garter st, work rows 1–8 of Purled Ladder Stitch patt over rem sts.

Rep rows 1–8 another 3 (6) times and then work rows 1–4 once more for a total of 36 (60) patt rows.

Inc row: K7 (11), M1, K14 (22), M1, K7 (11)— 30 (46) sts.

Knit 5 (9) rows.

BO kw on RS.

Broken Rib

Stitch Pattern

Multiple of 2 sts + 1 st

Row 1 (RS): Knit.

Row 2: P1, *K1, P1; rep from * to end.

Rep these 2 rows for patt.

Making a Block

To make Small (Large) block with border:

CO 30 (46) sts.

Knit 5 (9) rows.

Dec row: K14 (22), K2tog, K14 (22)—29 (45) sts.

Keeping first and last 3 (5) sts in garter st, work rows 1 and 2 of Broken Rib patt over rem sts.

Rep rows 1 and 2 another 17 (29) times for a total of 36 (60) patt rows.

Inc row: K14 (22), M1, K15 (23)—30 (46) sts.

Knit 5 (9) rows.

BO kw on RS.

Farrow Rib

Stitch Pattern

Multiple of 3 sts + 1 st

Row 1 (RS): *K2, P1; rep from * to last st, K1.

Row 2: P1, *K2, P1; rep from * to end.

Rep these 2 rows for patt.

Making a Block

To make Small (Large) block with border:

CO 30 (46) sts.

Knit 5 (9) rows.

Dec row: K8 (13), K2tog, K10 (16), K2tog, K8 (13)—28 (44) sts.

Keeping first and last 3 (5) sts in garter st, work rows 1 and 2 of Farrow Rib patt over rem sts.

Rep rows 1 and 2 another 17 (29) times for a total of 36 (60) patt rows.

Inc row: K7 (11), M1, K14 (22), M1, K7 (11)—30 (46) sts.

Knit 5 (9) rows.

BO kw on RS.

Box Stitch

Stitch Pattern

Multiple of 4 sts + 2 sts

Row 1 (RS): K2, *P2, K2; rep from * to end.

Row 2: P2, *K2, P2; rep from * to end.

Row 3: Rep row 2.

Row 4: Rep row 1.

Rep these 4 rows for patt.

Making a Block

To make Small (Large) block with border:

CO 30 (46) sts.

Knit 5 (9) rows.

Dec row: K8 (13), K2tog, K10 (16), K2tog, K8 (13)—28 (44) sts.

Keeping first and last 3 (5) sts in garter st, work rows 1–4 of Box Stitch patt over rem sts.

Rep rows 1–4 another 8 (14) times for a total of 36 (60) patt rows.

Inc row: K7 (11), M1, K14 (22), M1, K7 (11)—30 (46) sts.

Knit 5 (9) rows.

BO kw on RS.

Double Basket Weave

Stitch Pattern

Multiple of 4 sts + 3 sts

Row 1 and all odd-numbered rows (RS): Knit.

Row 2: *K3, P1; rep from * to last 3 sts, K3.

Row 4: Rep row 2.

Row 6: K1, *P1, K3; rep from * to last 2 sts, P1, K1.

Row 8: Rep row 6.

Rep these 8 rows for patt.

Making a Block

To make Small (Large) block with border:

CO 30 (46) sts.

Knit 5 (9) rows.

Dec row: K14 (22), K2tog, K14 (22)—29 (45) sts.

Keeping first and last 3 (5) sts in garter st, work rows 1–8 of Double Basket Weave patt over rem sts.

Rep rows 1–8 another 3 (6) times and then work rows 1–4 once more for a total of 36 (60) patt rows.

Inc row: K15 (23), M1, K14 (22)—30 (46) sts.

Knit 5 (9) rows.

BO kw on RS.

Tile Stitch

Stitch Pattern

Multiple of 6 sts + 4 sts

Rows 1, 3, and 5 (RS): K4, *P2, K4; rep from * to end.

Rows 2, 4, and 6: P4, *K2, P4; rep from * to end.

Row 7: P4, *K2, P4; rep from * to end.

Row 8: K4, *P2, K4; rep from * to end.

Rep these 8 rows for patt.

Making a Block

To make Small (Large) block with border:

CO 30 (46) sts.

Knit 5 (9) rows.

Dec row: K8 (13), K2tog, K10 (16), K2tog, K8 (13)—28 (44) sts.

Keeping first and last 3 (5) sts in garter st, work rows 1–8 of Tile Stitch patt over rem sts.

Rep rows 1–8 another 3 (6) times and then work rows 1–4 once more for a total of 36 (60) pattern rows.

Inc row: K7 (11), M1, K14 (22), M1, K7 (11)—30 (46) sts.

Knit 5 (9) rows.

BO kw on RS.

Banded Basket Stitch

Stitch Pattern

Multiple of 9 sts + 6 sts

Rows 1, 3, and 5 (RS): P6, *K3, P6; rep from * to end.

Rows 2, 4, and 6: K6, *P3, K6; rep from * to end.

Rows 7 and 9: K6, *P3, K6; rep from * to end.

Rows 8 and 10: P6, *K3, P6; rep from * to end.

Rep these 10 rows for patt.

Making a Block

To make Small (Large) block with border:

CO 30 (46) sts.

Knit 6 (9) rows.

Dec row (Large only): K10, K2tog, K10, K2tog, K10, K2tog, K10—43 sts.

Keeping first and last 3 (5) sts in garter st, work rows 1–10 of Banded Basket Stitch patt over rem sts.

Rep rows 1–10 another 2 (5) times and then work rows 1–6 another 1 (0) time for a total of 36 (60) patt rows.

Inc row (Large only): K11, M1, K11, M1, K11, M1, K10—46 sts.

Knit 6 (9) rows.

BO kw on RS.

Garter-Stitch Steps

Stitch Pattern

Multiple of 8 sts

Row 1 and all odd-numbered rows (RS): Knit.

Rows 2 and 4: *K4, P4; rep from * to end.

Rows 6 and 8: K2, *P4, K4; rep from * to last 6 sts, P4, K2.

Rows 10 and 12: *P4, K4; rep from * to end.

Rows 14 and 16: P2, *K4, P4; rep from * to last 6 sts, K4, P2.

Rep these 16 rows for patt.

Making a Block

To make Small (Large) block with border:

CO 30 (46) sts.

Knit 6 (9) rows.

Dec row (Large only): K5, K2tog, K9, K2tog, K10, K2tog, K9, K2tog, K5—42 sts.

Keeping first and last 3 (5) sts in garter st, work rows 1–16 of Garter-Stitch Steps patt over rem sts.

Rep rows 1–16 another 1 (2) time and then work rows 1–4 (1–12) once more for a total of 36 (60) patt rows.

Inc row (Large only): K7, M1, K11, M1, K6, M1, K11, M1, K7—46 sts.

Knit 6 (9) rows.

BO kw on RS.

Rectangular Checks

Stitch Pattern

Multiple of 6 sts

Row 1 and all odd-numbered rows (RS): Knit.

Rows 2, 4, 6, 8, 10, and 12: *K3, P3; rep from * to end.

Rows 14, 16, 18, 20, 22, and 24: *P3, K3; rep from * to end.

Rep these 24 rows for patt.

Making a Block

To make Small (Large) block with border:

CO 30 (46) sts.

Knit 6 (10) rows.

Keeping first and last 3 (5) sts in garter st, work rows 1–24 of Rectangular Checks patt over rem sts.

Rep rows 1–12 (1–24) once and then for *Large block only,* work rows 1–12 once more for a total of 36 (60) patt rows.

Knit 6 (10) rows.

BO kw on RS.

Harris-Tweed Rib

Stitch Pattern

Multiple of 4 sts + 2 sts

Row 1 (RS): K2, *P2, K2; rep from * to end.

Row 2: P2, *K2, P2; rep from * to end.

Row 3: Knit.

Row 4: Purl.

Row 5: Rep row 1.

Row 6: Rep row 2.

Row 7: Purl.

Row 8: Knit.

Rep these 8 rows for patt.

Making a Block

To make Small (Large) block with border:

CO 30 (46) sts.

Knit 5 (9) rows.

Inc row: K5 (8), *K5 (8), M1, K5 (7); rep from * once more, K5 (8)—32 (48) sts.

Keeping first and last 3 (5) sts in garter st, work rows 1–8 of Harris-Tweed Rib patt over rem sts.

Rep rows 1–8 another 3 (6) times and then rows 1–4 once more for a total of 36 (60) patt rows.

Dec row: K5 (8), *K4 (7), K2tog, K5 (7); rep from * once more, K5 (8)—30 (46) sts.

Knit 5 (9) rows.

BO kw on RS.

Zigzag Stitch

Stitch Pattern

Multiple of 6 sts

Row 1 (RS): *K3, P3; rep from * to end.

Row 2 and all even-numbered rows: Purl.

Row 3: P1, *K3, P3; rep from * to last 5 sts, K3, P2.

Row 5: P2, *K3, P3; rep from * to last 4 sts, K3, P1.

Row 7: *P3, K3; rep from * to end.

Row 9: Rep row 5.

Row 11: Rep row 3.

Row 12: Purl.

Rep these 12 rows for patt.

Making a Block

To make Small (Large) block with border:

CO 30 (46) sts.

Knit 6 (10) rows.

Keeping first and last 3 (5) sts in garter st, work rows 1–12 of Zigzag Stitch patt over rem sts.

Rep rows 1–12 another 2 (4) times for a total of 36 (60) patt rows.

Knit 6 (10) rows.

BO kw on RS.

Diagonal Rib 2

Stitch Pattern

Multiple of 4 sts

Rows 1 and 2: *K2, P2; rep from * to end.

Row 3 (RS): K1, *P2, K2; rep from * to last 3 sts, P2, K1.

Row 4: P1, *K2, P2; rep from * to last 3 sts, K2, P1.

Rows 5 and 6: *P2, K2; rep from * to end.

Row 7: Rep row 4.

Row 8: Rep row 5.

Rep these 8 rows for patt.

Making a Block

To make Small (Large) block with border:

CO 30 (46) sts.

Knit 6 (10) rows.

Keeping first and last 3 (5) sts in garter st, work rows 1–8 of Diagonal Rib 2 patt over rem sts.

Rep rows 1–8 another 3 (6) times and then work rows 1–4 once more for a total of 36 (60) patt rows.

Knit 6 (10) rows.

BO kw on RS.

Broken-Rib Diagonal

Stitch Pattern

Multiple of 6 sts

Rows 1 and 3 (RS): *K4, P2; rep from * to end.

Rows 2 and 4: *K2, P4; rep from * to end.

Rows 5 and 7: K2, *P2, K4; rep from * to last 4 sts, P2, K2.

Rows 6 and 8: P2, *K2, P4; rep from * to last 4 sts, K2, P2.

Rows 9 and 11: *P2, K4; rep from * to end.

Rows 10 and 12: *P4, K2; rep from * to end.

Rep these 12 rows for patt.

Making a Block

To make Small (Large) block with border:

CO 30 (46) sts.

Knit 6 (10) rows.

Keeping first and last 3 (5) sts in garter st, work rows 1–12 of Broken-Rib Diagonal patt over rem sts.

Rep rows 1–12 another 2 (4) times for a total of 36 (60) patt rows.

Knit 6 (10) rows.

BO kw on RS.

Sailors' Rib

Stitch Pattern

Multiple of 5 sts + 1 st

Row 1 (RS): K1tbl, *P1, K2, P1, K1tbl; rep from * to end.

Row 2: P1, *K1, P2, K1, P1; rep from * to end.

Row 3: K1tbl, *P4, K1tbl; rep from * to end.

Row 4: P1, *K4, P1; rep from * to end.

Rep these 4 rows for patt.

Making a Block

To make Small (Large) block with border:

CO 30 (46) sts.

Knit 5 (10) rows.

Inc row (Small only): K9, M1, K12, M1, K9—32 sts.

Keeping first and last 3 (5) sts in garter st, work rows 1–4 of Sailors' Rib patt over rem sts.

Rep rows 1–4 another 8 (14) times for a total of 36 (60) patt rows.

Dec row (Small only): K9, K2tog, K9, K2tog, K10—30 sts.

Knit 5 (10) rows.

BO kw on RS.

Embossed Check Stitch

Stitch Pattern

Multiple of 2 sts + 1 st

Row 1 (RS): K1tbl across.

Row 2: K1, *P1tbl, K1; rep from * to end.

Row 3: P1, *K1tbl, P1; rep from * to end.

Row 4: Rep row 2.

Row 5: Rep row 1.

Row 6: P1tbl, *K1, P1tbl; rep from * to end.

Row 7: K1tbl, *P1, K1tbl; rep from * to end.

Row 8: Rep row 6.

Rep these 8 rows for patt.

Making a Block

To make Small (Large) block with border:

CO 30 (46) sts.

Knit 5 (9) rows.

Dec row: K14 (22), K2tog, K14 (22)—29 (45) sts.

Keeping first and last 3 (5) sts in garter st, work rows 1–8 of Embossed Check Stitch patt over rem sts.

Rep rows 1–8 another 3 (6) times and then work rows 1–4 once more for a total of 36 (60) patt rows.

Inc row: K15 (23), M1, K14 (22)—30 (46) sts.

Knit 5 (9) rows.

BO kw on RS.

Double Woven Stitch

Stitch Pattern

Multiple of 4 sts

Row 1 (RS): K3, *sl 2 wyif, K2; rep from * to last st, K1.

Row 2: Purl.

Row 3: K1, *sl 2 wyif, K2; rep from * to last 3 sts, sl 2 wyif, K1.

Row 4: Purl.

Rep these 4 rows for patt.

Making a Block

To make Small (Large) block with border:

CO 30 (46) sts.

Knit 6 (10) rows.

Keeping first and last 3 (5) sts in garter st, work rows 1–4 of Double Woven Stitch patt over rem sts.

Rep rows 1–4 another 8 (14) times for a total of 36 (60) patt rows.

Knit 6 (10) rows.

BO kw on RS.

Rose-Hip Stitch

Stitch Pattern

Multiple of 4 sts + 3 sts

Row 1 (RS): K3, *sl 1 wyib, K3; rep from * to end.

Row 2: K3, *sl 1 wyif, K3; rep from * to end.

Row 3: K1, *sl 1 wyib, K3; rep from * to last 2 sts, sl 1 wyib, K1.

Row 4: K1, *sl 1 wyif, K3; rep from * to last 2 sts, sl 1 wyif, K1.

Rep these 4 rows for patt.

Making a Block

To make Small (Large) block with border:

CO 30 (46) sts.

Knit 5 (9) rows.

Dec row: K14 (22), K2tog, K14 (22)—29 (45) sts.

Keeping first and last 3 (5) sts in garter st, work rows 1–4 of Rose-Hip Stitch patt over rem sts.

Rep rows 1–4 another 8 (14) times for a total of 36 (60) patt rows.

Inc row: K14 (22), M1, K15 (23) sts.

Knit 5 (9) rows.

BO kw on RS.

Double Mock Rib

Stitch Pattern

Multiple of 4 sts + 2 sts

Row 1 (RS): K2, *P2, K2; rep from * to end.

Row 2: P2, *sl 2 wyif, P2; rep from * to end.

Rep these 2 rows for patt.

Making a Block

To make Small (Large) block with border:

CO 30 (46) sts.

Knit 5 (9) rows.

Inc row: K12 (18), M1, K6 (10), M1, K12 (18)— 32 (48) sts.

Keeping first and last 3 (5) sts in garter st, work rows 1 and 2 of Double Mock Rib patt over rem sts.

Rep rows 1 and 2 another 17 (29) times for a total of 36 (60) patt rows.

Dec row: K11 (17), K2tog, K6 (10), K2tog, K11 (17)— 30 (46) sts.

K5 (9) rows.

BO kw on RS.

Lattice Stitch

Stitch Pattern

Multiple of 6 sts + 1 st

Row 1 (RS): K3, *P1, K5; rep from * to last 4 sts, P1, K3.

Row 2: P2, *K1, P1, K1, P3; rep from * to last 5 sts, K1, P1, K1, P2.

Row 3: K1, *P1, K3, P1, K1; rep from * to end.

Row 4: K1, *P5, K1; rep from * to end.

Row 5: Rep row 3.

Row 6: Rep row 2.

Rep these 6 rows for patt.

Making a Block

To make Small (Large) block with border:

CO 30 (46) sts.

Knit 5 (9) rows.

Inc row: K15 (23), M1, K15 (23)—31 (47) sts.

Keeping first and last 3 (5) sts in garter st, work rows 1–6 of Lattice Stitch patt over rem sts.

Rep rows 1–6 another 5 (9) times for a total of 36 (60) patt rows.

Dec row: K15 (23), K2tog, K14 (22)—30 (46) sts.

Knit 5 (9) rows.

BO kw on RS.

Seed-Stitch Checks

Stitch Pattern

Multiple of 10 sts + 5 sts

Rows 1, 3, and 5 (RS): K5, *(P1, K1) twice, P1, K5; rep from * to end.

Rows 2 and 4: P6, *K1, P1, K1, P7; rep from * to last 9 sts, K1, P1, K1, P6.

Rows 6 and 8: *(K1, P1) twice, K1, P5; rep from * to last 5 sts, (K1, P1) twice, K1.

Rows 7 and 9: (K1, P1) twice, *K7, P1, K1, P1; rep from * to last st, K1.

Row 10: Rep row 6.

Rep these 10 rows for patt.

Making a Block

To make Small (Large) block with border:

CO 30 (46) sts.

Knit 5 (9) rows.

Inc/dec row: K15 (22), M1 (K2tog), K15 (22)—31 (45) sts.

Keeping first and last 3 (5) sts in garter st, work rows 1–10 of Seed-Stitch Checks patt over rem sts.

Rep rows 1–10 another 2 (5) times.

Small only: Work rows 1–5 once more, and then work row 4 again.

Dec/inc row (both sizes): K14 (22), K2tog (M1), K15 (23)—30 (46) sts.

Knit 5 (9) rows.

BO kw on WS.

King Charles Brocade

Making a Block

To make Small (Large) block with border:

CO 30 (46) sts.

Knit 5 (9) rows.

Inc row: K15 (23), M1, K15 (23)—31 (47) sts.

Keeping first and last 3 (5) sts in garter st, work rows 1–12 of King Charles Brocade patt over rem sts.

Rep rows 1–12 another 2 (4) times for a total of 36 (60) patt rows.

Dec row: K15 (23), K2tog, K14 (22)—30 (46) sts.

Knit 5 (9) rows.

BO kw on RS.

Stitch Pattern

Multiple of 12 sts + 1 st

Row 1 (RS): K1, *P1, K9, P1, K1; rep from * to end.

Row 2: K1, P1, K1, *P7, (K1, P1) twice, K1; rep from * to last 10 sts, P7, K1, P1, K1.

Row 3: (K1, P1) twice, *K5, (P1, K1) 3 times, P1; rep from * to last 9 sts, K5 (P1, K1) twice.

Row 4: P2, *K1, P1, K1, P3; rep from * to last 5 sts, K1, P1, K1, P2.

Row 5: K3, *(P1, K1) 3 times, P1, K5; rep from * to last 10 sts, (P1, K1) 3 times, P1, K3.

Row 6: P4, *(K1, P1) twice, K1, P7; rep from * to last 9 sts, (K1, P1) twice, K1, P4.

Row 7: K5, *P1, K1, P1, K9; rep from * to last 8 sts, P1, K1, P1, K5.

Row 8: Rep row 6.

Row 9: Rep row 5.

Row 10: Rep row 4.

Row 11: Rep row 3.

Row 12: Rep row 2.

Rep these 12 rows for patt.

Reverse Stockinette Chevron

Stitch Pattern

Multiple of 6 sts + 5 sts

Row 1 (RS): K5, *P1, K5; rep from * to end.

Row 2: K1, *P3, K3; rep from * to last 4 sts, P3, K1.

Row 3: P2, *K1, P2; rep from * to end.

Row 4: P1, *K3, P3; rep from * to last 4 sts, K3, P1.

Row 5: K2, *P1, K5; rep from * to last 3 sts, P1, K2.

Row 6: Purl.

Rep these 6 rows for patt.

Making a Block

To make Small (Large) block with border:

CO 30 (46) sts.

Knit 5 (9) rows.

Dec row: K14 (22), K2tog, K14 (22)—29 (45) sts.

Keeping first and last 3 (5) sts in garter st, work rows 1–6 of Reverse Stockinette Chevron patt over rem sts.

Rep rows 1–6 another 5 (9) times for a total of 36 (60) patt rows.

Inc row: K15 (23), M1, K14 (22)—30 (46) sts.

Knit 5 (9) rows.

BO kw on RS.

Ridged Eyelet Border

Stitch Pattern

Multiple of 2 sts + 1 st

Rows 1–3: Knit.

Row 4 (WS): *P2 tog, YO; rep from * to last st, P1.

Rows 5–7: Knit.

Row 8: Purl.

Rows 9–16: Rep rows 1–8.

Rows 17 and 19: Knit.

Rows 18 and 20: Purl.

Rep these 20 rows for patt.

Making a Block

To make Small (Large) block with border:

CO 30 (46) sts.

Knit 5 (9) rows.

Inc row: K15 (23), M1, K15 (23)—31 (47) sts.

Set-up row 1 (RS): K3 (5), K25 (37), K3 (5).

Set-up row 2: K3 (5), P25 (37), K3 (5).

Keeping first and last 3 (5) sts in garter st, work rows 1–20 of Ridged Eyelet Border patt over rem sts.

Rep rows 1–14 (1–20) once more.

Large only: Rep rows 1–18 once more.

Dec row (both sizes): K15 (23), K2tog, K14 (22)—30 (46) sts.

Knit 5 (9) rows.

BO kw on RS.

Open Check Stitch

Stitch Pattern

Multiple of 2 sts

Row 1 (RS): Purl.

Row 2: Knit.

Row 3: K2, *sl 1, K1; rep from * to end.

Row 4: *K1, sl 1 wyif; rep from * to last 2 sts, K2.

Row 5: K1, *YO, K2tog; rep from * to last st, K1.

Row 6: Purl.

Rep these 6 rows for patt.

Making a Block

To make Small (Large) block with border:

CO 30 (46) sts.

Knit 6 (10) rows.

Keeping first and last 3 (5) sts in garter st, work rows 1–6 of Open Check Stitch patt over rem sts.

Rep rows 1–6 another 5 (9) times for a total of 36 (60) patt rows.

Knit 6 (10) rows.

BO kw on RS.

Ridged Lace 1

Stitch Pattern

Multiple of 2 sts + 1 st

Rows 1–3: Purl.

Row 4 (RS): K1, *YO, sl 1, K1, psso; rep from * to end.

Rows 5–7: Purl.

Row 8: K1, *YO, K2tog; rep from * to end.

Rep these 8 rows for patt.

Making a Block

For Small (Large) block with border:

CO 30 (46) sts.

Knit 6 (10) rows.

Dec row (RS): K8 (13), K2tog, K4 (7), K2tog, K4 (7), K2tog, K8 (13)—27 (43) sts.

Keeping first and last 3 (5) sts in garter st, work rows 1–8 of Ridged Lace 1 patt over rem sts.

Rep rows 1–8 another 3 (6) times and then work rows 1–3 once more.

Inc row (RS): K9 (14), M1, K5 (8), M1, K5 (8), M1, K8 (13)—30 (46) sts.

Knit 5 (9) rows.

BO kw on RS.

Eyelets

Stitch Pattern

Multiple of 3 sts + 2 sts

Row 1 (RS): Knit.

Row 2: Purl.

Row 3: K2, *YO, K2tog, K1; rep from * to end.

Row 4: Purl.

Rep these 4 rows for patt.

Making a Block

To make Small (Large) block with border:

CO 30 (46) sts.

Knit 5 (9) rows.

Dec row: K3 (5), K2tog, K5 (9), K2tog, K6 (10), K2tog, K5 (9), K2tog, K3 (5)—26 (42) sts.

Keeping first and last 3 (5) sts in garter st, work rows 1–4 of Eyelets patt over rem sts.

Rep rows 1–4 another 8 (14) times for a total of 36 (60) patt rows.

Inc row: K3 (5), M1, K7 (11), M1, K6 (10), M1, K7 (11), M1, K3 (5)—30 (46) sts.

Knit 5 (9) rows.

BO kw on RS.

Stockinette Ridge

Stitch Pattern

Multiple of 2 sts

Row 1 (RS): Knit.

Row 2: P1, *K2tog; rep from * to last st, P1.

Row 3: K1, *K1f&b; rep from * to last st, K1.

Row 4: Purl.

Rep these 4 rows for patt.

Making a Block

To make Small (Large) block with border:

CO 30 (46) sts.

Knit 6 (10) rows.

Keeping first and last 3 (5) sts in garter st, work rows 1–4 of Stockinette Ridge patt over rem sts.

Rep rows 1–4 another 8 (14) times for a total of 36 (60) patt rows.

Knit 6 (10) rows.

BO kw on RS.

Bamboo Stitch

Stitch Pattern

Multiple of 2 sts

Row 1 (RS): *YO, K2, pass YO over K2; rep from * to end.

Row 2: Purl.

Rep these 2 rows for patt.

Making a Block

To make Small (Large) block with border:

CO 30 (46) sts.

Knit 6 (10) rows.

Keeping first and last 3 (5) sts in garter st, work rows 1 and 2 of Bamboo Stitch patt over rem sts.

Rep rows 1 and 2 another 17 (29) times and then work row 1 once more.

Knit 5 (9) rows.

BO kw on RS.

Crocus Buds

Stitch Pattern

Multiple of 2 sts + 1 st

Row 1 (RS): K1, *YO, K2; rep from * to end.

Row 2: P1, *P3, pass 3rd st on right-hand needle over 2 sts; rep from * to end.

Row 3: *K2, YO; rep from * to last st, K1.

Row 4: *P3, pass 3rd st on right-hand needle over first 2 sts; rep from * to last st, P1.

Rep these 4 rows for patt.

Making a Block

To make Small (Large) block with border:

CO 30 (46) sts.

Knit 5 (9) rows.

Dec row: K6 (7), K2tog, *K6 (4), K2tog, K6 (3), K2tog, K3 (4); rep from * 0 (1) times, K3 (5)—27 (41) sts.

Keeping first and last 3 (5) sts in garter st, work rows 1–4 of Crocus Buds patt over rem sts.

Rep rows 1–4 another 8 (14) times for a total of 36 (60) patt rows.

Inc row: K6 (10), M1, *K7 (5), M1, K7 (5), M1, K4 (3); rep from * 0 (1) times, K3 (5)—30 (46) sts.

Knit 5 (9) more rows.

BO kw on RS.

Cluster Rib

Stitch Pattern

Multiple of 3 sts + 1 st

Row 1 (RS): P1, *K2, P1; rep from * to end.

Row 2: K1, *YO, K2, slip YO over the 2 knit sts, K1; rep from * to end.

Rep these 2 rows for patt.

Making a Block

To make Small (Large) block with border:

CO 30 (46) sts.

Knit 5 (9) rows.

Inc row: K15 (23), M1, K15 (23)—31 (47) sts.

Keeping first and last 3 (5) sts in garter st, work rows 1 and 2 of Cluster Rib patt over rem sts.

Rep rows 1 and 2 another 17 (29) times for a total of 36 (60) patt rows.

Dec row: K15 (23), K2tog, K14 (22)—30 (46) sts.

Knit 5 (9) rows.

BO kw on RS.

Simple Garter-Stitch Lace

Stitch Pattern

Multiple of 4 sts + 2 sts

All rows: K2, *YO, P2tog, K2; rep from * to end.

Rep this row for patt.

Making a Block

To make Small (Large) block with border:

CO 30 (46) sts.

Knit 5 (9) rows.

Dec row: [K3 (5), K2tog] twice, [K2 (5), K2tog] 3 times, K3 (4), K2tog, K3 (5)—24 (40) sts.

Keeping first and last 3 (5) sts in garter st, work row 1 of Simple Garter-Stitch Lace patt over rem sts.

Rep row 1 another 35 (59) times for a total of 36 (60) patt rows.

Inc row: K4 (7), M1, K4 (5), M1, K3 (5), M1, K2 (6), M1, K3 (5), M1, K4 (5), M1, K4 (7)—30 (46) sts.

Knit 5 (9) rows.

BO kw on RS.

Blanket Rib

Stitch Pattern

Multiple of 2 sts + 1 st

Row 1 (RS): K1f&b in each st (thus doubling the number of sts).

Row 2: K2tog, *P2tog, K2tog; rep from * to end (original number of sts restored).

Rep these 2 rows for patt.

Making a Block

To make Small (Large) block with border:

CO 30 (46) sts.

Knit 5 (9) rows.

Dec row: K5 (6), K2tog, [K7 (6), K2tog] 2 (4) times, K5 (6)—27 (41) sts.

Keeping first and last 3 (5) sts in garter st, work rows 1 and 2 of Blanket Rib patt over rem sts.

Rep rows 1 and 2 another 17 (29) times for a total of 36 (60) patt rows.

Inc row: K4 (8), M1, [K9 (6), M1] 2 (4) times, K5 (9)—30 (46) sts.

Knit 5 (9) rows.

BO kw on RS.

Blanket Moss Stitch

Stitch Pattern

Multiple of 2 sts + 1 st

Note: Count stitches after rows 2 and 4 only, as stitch count does change.

Rows 1 and 3 (RS): K1f&b in each st (thus doubling the number of sts).

Row 2: K2tog, *P2tog, K2tog; rep from * to end (original number of sts restored).

Row 4: P2tog, *K2tog, P2tog; rep from * to end (original number of sts restored).

Rep these 4 rows for patt.

Making a Block

To make Small (Large) block with border:

CO 30 (46) sts.

Knit 5 (9) rows.

Dec row: K4 (5), K2tog, *K3, K2tog; rep from * to last 4 (5) sts, K4 (5)—25 (39) sts.

Keeping first and last 3 (5) sts in garter st, work rows 1–4 of Blanket Moss Stitch patt over rem sts.

Rep rows 1–4 another 8 (14) times for a total of 36 (60) patt rows.

Inc row: K4 (5), M1, *K4, M1; rep from * to last 5 sts, K5—30 (46) sts.

Knit 5 (9) rows.

BO kw on RS.

Bramble Stitch

Stitch Pattern

Multiple of 4 sts + 2 sts

Row 1 (RS): Purl.

Row 2: K1, *(K1, P1, K1) into next st, P3tog; rep from * to last st, K1.

Row 3: Purl.

Row 4: K1, *P3tog, (K1, P1, K1) into next st; rep from * to last st, K1.

Rep these 4 rows for patt.

Making a Block

To make Small (Large) block with border:

CO 30 (46) sts.

Knit 5 (9) rows.

Dec row: K8 (13), K2tog, K10 (16), K2tog, K8 (13)— 28 (44) sts.

Keeping first and last 3 (5) sts in garter st, work rows 1–4 of Bramble Stitch patt over rem sts.

Rep rows 1–4 another 8 (14) times for a total of 36 (60) patt rows.

Inc row: K7 (11), M1, K14 (22), M1, K7 (11)— 30 (46) sts.

Knit 5 (9) rows.

BO kw on RS.

Garter Stitch Twisted Rib

Stitch Pattern

Multiple of 4 sts

Row 1 (RS): K1, *cross 2 back, K2; rep from * to last 3 sts, cross 2 back, K1.

Row 2: K1, *yf, cross 2 purl, yb, K2; rep from * to last 3 sts, yf, cross 2 purl, yb, K1.

Rep these 2 rows for patt.

Making a Block

To make Small (Large) block with border:

CO 30 (46) sts.

Knit 6 (10) rows.

Keeping first and last 3 (5) sts in garter st, work rows 1 and 2 of Garter Stitch Twisted Rib patt over rem sts.

Rep rows 1 and 2 another 17 (29) times for a total of 36 (60) patt rows.

Knit 6 (10) rows.

BO kw on RS.

Corded Rib

Stitch Pattern

Multiple of 4 sts + 2 sts

All rows: K1, *K2tog tbl, M1L, P2; rep from * to last st, K1.

Rep this row for patt.

Making a Block

To make Small (Large) block with border:

CO 30 (46) sts.

Knit 5 (9) rows.

Inc row, Small only (RS): K9, M1, K12, M1, K9— 32 sts.

Inc row, Large only (RS): K8, [K15, M1] twice, K8— 48 sts.

Keeping first and last 3 (5) sts in garter st, work row 1 of Corded Rib patt over rem sts.

Rep row 1 another 35 (59) times for a total of 36 (60) patt rows.

Dec row, Small only (RS): K9, K2tog, K10, K2tog, K9—30 sts.

Dec row, Large only (RS): K8, [K14, K2tog] twice, K8—46 sts.

Knit 5 (9) rows.

BO kw on RS.

Eyelet Lattice Insertion

Stitch Pattern

Worked over 8 sts on a background of St st

Row 1 (RS): K1, (K2tog, YO) 3 times, K1.

Rows 2 and 4: Purl.

Row 3: K2, (K2tog, YO) twice, K2.

Rep these 4 rows for patt.

Making a Block

To make Small (Large) block with border:

CO 30 (46) sts.

Knit 6 (10) rows.

Keeping first and last 3 (5) sts in garter st, work rem sts as follows:

Row 1: *K2, work row 1 of Eyelet Lattice Insertion patt over next 8 sts, K2; rep from * across row.

Row 2: *P2, work row 2 of Eyelet Lattice Insertion over next 8 sts, P2; rep from * across row.

Row 3: *K2, work row 3 of Eyelet Lattice Insertion over next 8 sts, K2; rep from * across row.

Row 4: *P2, work row 4 of Eyelet Lattice Insertion over next 8 sts, P2; rep from * across row.

Rep rows 1–4 another 8 (14) times for a total of 36 (60) patt rows.

Knit 6 (10) rows.

BO kw on RS.

Eyelet Twigs

Stitch Pattern

Worked over 14 sts on a background of St st

Row 1 (RS): K1, YO, K3tog, YO, K3, YO, sl 1, K2tog, psso, YO, K4.

Row 2 and all even-numbered rows: Purl.

Row 3: YO, K3tog, YO, K5, YO, sl 1, K2tog, psso, YO, K3.

Row 5: K5, YO, K3tog, YO, K1, YO, sl 1, K2tog, psso, YO, K2.

Row 7: K4, YO, K3tog, YO, K3, YO, sl 1, K2tog, psso, YO, K1.

Row 9: K3, YO, K3tog, YO, K5, YO, sl 1, K2tog, psso, YO.

Row 11: K2, YO, K3tog, YO, K1, YO, sl 1, K2tog, psso, YO, K5.

Row 12: Rep row 2.

Rep these 12 rows for patt.

Making a Block

To make Small (Large) block with border:

CO 30 (46 sts).

Knit 6 (10) rows.

Keeping first and last 3 (5) sts in garter st, work St st and Eyelet Twigs patt over rem 24 (36) sts as follows:

Row 1 (RS): K5 (2), *work row 1 of Eyelet Twigs patt**, K0 (4); rep from * to ** 0 (1) time, K5 (2).

Row 2: P5 (2), *work row 2 of Eyelet Twigs patt**, P0 (4); rep from * to ** 0 (1) time, P5 (2).

Row 3: K5 (2), *work row 3 of Eyelet Twigs patt**, K0 (4); rep from * to ** 0 (1) time, K5 (2).

Row 4: P5 (2), *work row 4 of Eyelet Twigs patt**, P0 (4); rep from * to ** 0 (1) time, P5 (2).

Row 5: K5 (2), *work row 5 of Eyelet Twigs patt**, K0 (4); rep from * to ** 0 (1) time, K5 (2).

Row 6: P5 (2), *work row 6 of Eyelet Twigs patt**, P0 (4); rep from * to ** 0 (1) time, P5 (2).

Row 7: K5 (2), *work row 7 of Eyelet Twigs patt**, K0 (4); rep from * to ** 0 (1) time, K5 (2).

Row 8: P5 (2), *work row 8 of Eyelet Twigs patt**, P0 (4); rep from * to ** 0 (1) time, P5 (2).

Row 9: K5 (2), *work row 9 of Eyelet Twigs patt**, K0 (4); rep from * to ** 0 (1) time, K5 (2).

Row 10: P5 (2), *work row 10 of Eyelet Twigs patt**, P0 (4); rep from * to ** 0 (1) time, P5 (2).

Row 11: K5 (2), *work row 11 of Eyelet Twigs patt**, K0 (4); rep from * to ** 0 (1) times, K5 (2).

Row 12: Rep row 2.

Rep rows 1–12 another 2 (4) times for a total of 36 (60) patt rows.

Knit 6 (10) rows.

BO kw on RS.

Vandyke Lace Panel 1

Stitch Pattern

Worked over 17 sts on a background of St st

Row 1 (RS): *K2tog, YO, K1, YO, sl 1, K1, psso**, K3, YO, sl 1, K1, psso, K2; rep from * to ** once more.

Rows 2 and 4: Purl.

Row 3: (K2tog, YO, K1, YO, sl 1, K1, psso, K1) twice, K2tog, YO, K1, YO, sl 1, K1, psso.

Row 5: *K2tog, YO, K1, YO, sl 1, K1, psso**, K2tog, YO, K3, YO, sl 1, K1, psso; rep from * to ** once more.

Row 6: Purl.

Rep these 6 rows for patt.

Making a Block

To make Small (Large) block with border:

CO 30 (46) sts.

Knit 5 (9) rows.

Dec row: K14 (22), K2tog, K14 (22)—29 (45) sts.

Keeping first and last 3 (5) sts in garter stitch, work rows 1–6 of Vandyke Lace Panel 1 patt over rem sts as follows:

Row 1: K3 (9), work row 1 of Vandyke Lace Panel 1 over next 17 sts, K3 (9).

Row 2: P3 (9), work row 2 of Vandyke Lace Panel 1 over next 17 sts, P3 (9).

Row 3: K3 (9), work row 3 of Vandyke Lace Panel 1 over next 17 sts, K3 (9).

Row 4: P3 (9), work row 4 of Vandyke Lace Panel 1 over next 17 sts, P3 (9).

Row 5: K3 (9), work row 5 of Vandyke Lace Panel 1 over next 17 sts, K3 (9).

Row 6: P3 (9), work row 6 of Vandyke Lace Panel 1 over next 17 sts, P3 (9).

Rep rows 1–6 another 5 (9) times for a total of 36 (60) patt rows.

Inc row: K14 (22), M1, K15 (23)—30 (46) sts.

Knit 5 (9) rows.

BO kw on RS.

Vandyke Lace Panel 2

Stitch Pattern

Worked over 9 sts on a background of St st

Row 1 (RS): K4, YO, sl 1, K1, psso, K3.

Row 2 and all even-numbered rows: Purl.

Row 3: K2, K2tog, YO, K1, YO, sl 1, K1, psso, K2.

Row 5: K1, K2tog, YO, K3, YO, sl 1, K1, psso, K1.

Row 7: K2tog, YO, K5, YO, sl 1, K1, psso.

Row 8: Purl.

Rep these 8 rows for patt.

Making a Block

To make Small (Large) block with border:

CO 30 (46) sts.

Knit 6 (10) rows.

Set-up row 1: Knit.

Set-up row 2: K3 (5), P24 (36), K3 (5).

Keeping first and last 3 (5) sts in garter st, work over rem sts as follows:

Row 1: K2 (3),*work row 1 of Vandyke Lace Panel 2 patt over next 9 sts, K2; rep from * across.

Row 2: *P2, work row 2 of Vandyke Lace Panel 2, P2; rep from * to last 2 (3) sts, P2 (3).

Row 3: K2 (3), *work row 3 of Vandyke Lace Panel 2, K2; rep from * across.

Row 4: *P2, work row 4 of Vandyke Lace Panel 2, P2; rep from * to last 2 (3) sts, P2 (3).

Row 5: K2 (3), *work row 5 of Vandyke Lace Panel 2, K2; rep from * across.

Row 6: *P2, work row 6 of Vandyke Lace Panel 2, P2; rep from * to last 2 (3) sts, P2 (3).

Row 7: K2 (3), *work row 7 of Vandyke Lace Panel 2, K2; rep from * across.

Row 8: *P2, work row 8 of Vandyke Lace Panel 2, K2; rep from * to last 2 (3) sts, P2 (3).

Rep rows 1–8 another 3 (6) times.

Work set-up rows 1 and 2.

Knit 6 (10) rows.

BO kw on RS.

Fish-Scale Lace Panel

Stitch Pattern

Worked over 17 sts on a background of St st

Row 1 (RS): K1, YO, K3, sl 1, K1, psso, P5, K2tog, K3, YO, K1.

Row 2: P6, K5, P6.

Row 3: K2, YO, K3, sl 1, K1, psso, P3, K2tog, K3, YO, K2.

Row 4: P7, K3, P7.

Row 5: K3, YO, K3, sl 1, K1, psso, P1, K2tog, K3, YO, K3.

Row 6: P8, K1, P8.

Row 7: K4, YO, K3, sl 1, K2tog, psso, K3, YO, K4.

Row 8: Purl.

Rep these 8 rows for patt.

Making a Block

To make a Small (Large) block with border:

CO 30 (46) sts.

Knit 5 (9) rows.

Dec row: K14 (22), K2tog, K14 (22)—29 (45 sts).

Set-up row 1: Knit.

Set-up row 2: K3 (5), P23 (35), K3 (5).

Keeping first and last 3 (5) sts in garter st, work Fish-Scale Lace Panel as follows:

Row 1 (RS): K3 (9), work row 1 of Fish-Scale Lace Panel, K3 (9).

Row 2: P3 (9), work row 2 of Fish-Scale Lace Panel, P3 (9).

Row 3: K3 (9), work row 3 of Fish-Scale Lace Panel, K3 (9).

Row 4: P3 (9), work row 4 of Fish-Scale Lace Panel, P3 (9).

Row 5: K3 (9), work row 5 of Fish-Scale Lace Panel, K3 (9).

Row 6: P3 (9), work row 6 of Fish-Scale Lace Panel, P3 (9).

Row 7: K3 (9), work row 7 of Fish-Scale Lace Panel, K3 (9).

Row 8: P3 (9), work row 8 of Fish-Scale Lace Panel, P3 (9).

Rep rows 1–8 another 3 (6) times

Rep set-up rows 1 and 2.

Inc row: K14 (22), M1, K15 (23)—30 (46) sts.

K5 (9) rows.

BO kw on RS.

Single Lace Rib

Stitch Pattern

Multiple of 4 sts + 1 st

Row 1 (RS): K1, *YO, K2tog, P1, K1; rep from * to end.

Row 2: P1, *YO, P2tog, K1, P1; rep from * to end.

Rep these 2 rows for patt.

Making a Block

To make Small (Large) block with border:

CO 30 (46) sts.

Knit 5 (9) rows.

Dec row: K5 (6), K2tog, *K7 (6), K2tog; rep from * to last 5 (6) sts, K5 (6)—27 (41) sts.

Keeping first and last 3 (5) sts in garter st, work rows 1 and 2 of Single Lace Rib patt.

Rep rows 1 and 2 another 17 (29) times for a total of 36 (60) patt rows.

Inc row: K4 (7), M1, *K9 (7), M1; rep from * to last 5 (6) sts, K5 (6)—30 (46) sts.

Knit 5 (9) rows.

BO kw on RS.

Double Lace Rib

Stitch Pattern

Multiple of 6 sts + 2 sts

Row 1 (RS): K2, *P1, YO, K2tog tbl, P1, K2; rep from * to end.

Row 2: P2, *K1, P2; rep from * to end.

Row 3: K2, *P1, K2tog, YO, P1, K2; rep from * to end.

Row 4: Rep row 2.

Rep these 4 rows for patt.

Making a Block

To make Small (Large) block with border:

CO 30 (46) sts.

Knit 5 (9) rows.

Dec row: K3 (5), K2tog, K5 (9), K2tog, K6 (10), K2tog, K5 (9), K2tog, K3 (5)—26 (42) sts.

Keeping first and last 3 (5) sts in garter st, work rows 1–4 of Double Lace Rib patt over rem sts.

Rep rows 1–4 another 8 (14) times for a total of 36 (60) patt rows.

Inc row: K3 (5), M1, K7 (11), M1, K6 (10), M1, K7 (11), M1, K3 (5)—30 (46) sts.

Knit 5 (9) rows.

BO kw on RS.

Perforated Ribbing

Stitch Pattern

Multiple of 6 sts + 3 sts

Row 1 (RS): P1, K1, P1, *YO, P3tog, YO, P1, K1, P1; rep from * to end.

Row 2: K1, P1, K1, *P3, K1, P1, K1; rep from * to end.

Row 3: P1, K1, P1, *K3, P1, K1, P1; rep from * to end.

Row 4: Rep row 2.

Rep these 4 rows for patt.

Making a Block

To make Small (Large) block with border:

CO 30 (46) sts.

Knit 5 (9) rows.

Dec row: K6 (10), K2tog, K6 (10), K2tog, K6 (10), K2tog, K6 (10)—27 (43) sts

Keeping first and last 3 (5) sts in garter st, work rows 1–4 of Perforated Ribbing patt over rem sts.

Rep rows 1–4 another 8 (14) times for a total of 36 (60) patt rows.

Inc row: K7 (11), M1, K7 (11), M1, K7 (11), M1, K6 (10)—30 (46) sts.

Knit 5 (9) rows.

BO kw on RS.

Single-Eyelet Rib

Stitch Pattern

Multiple of 5 sts + 2 sts

Row 1 (RS): P2, *K3, P2; rep from * to end.

Rows 2, 4, and 6: K2, *P3, K2; rep from * to end.

Row 3: P2, *K2tog, YO, K1, P2; rep from * to end.

Row 5: Rep row 1.

Row 7: P2, *K1, YO, sl 1, K1, psso, P2; rep from * to end.

Row 8: Rep row 2.

Rep these 8 rows for patt.

Making a Block

To make a Small (Large) block with border:

CO 30 (46) sts.

Knit 5 (9) rows.

Dec row: K8 (14), K2tog, K10 (14), K2tog, K8 (14)—28 (44) sts.

Keeping first and last 3 (5) sts in garter st, work rows 1–8 of Single-Eyelet Rib over rem sts.

Rep rows 1–8 another 3 (7) times. Work rows 1–4 once more for a total of 36 (60) patt rows.

Inc row: K7 (13), M1, K14 (18), M1, K7 (13)—30 (46) sts

Knit 5 (9) rows.

BO kw on RS.

Bobble Rib

Stitch Pattern

Multiple of 8 sts + 3 sts

Row 1 (RS): K3, *P2, (P1, K1) twice into next st, pass the first 3 of these sts, one at a time, over the 4th st (bobble made), P2, K3; rep from * to end.

Row 2: P3, *K2, P1, K2, P3; rep from * to end.

Row 3: K3, *P2, K1, P2, K3; rep from * to end.

Row 4: Rep row 2.

Rep these 4 rows for patt.

Making a Block

To make Small (Large) block with border:

CO 30 (46) sts.

Knit 5 (9) rows.

Inc row, Small only: K9, M1, K6, M1, K6, M1, K9—33 sts.

Dec row, Large only: K22, K2tog, K22—45 sts.

Keeping first and last 3 (5) sts in garter st, work rows 1–4 of Bobble Rib patt over rem sts.

Rep rows 1–4 another 8 (14) times for a total of 36 (60) patt rows.

Dec row, Small only: K8, K2tog, K5, K2tog, K6, K2tog, K8—30 sts.

Inc row, Large only: K22, M1, K23—46 sts.

Knit 5 (9) rows.

BO kw on RS.

Lacy Openwork

Stitch Pattern

Multiple of 4 sts + 1 st

Row 1 (RS): K1, *YO, P3tog, YO, K1; rep from * to end.

Row 2: P2tog, YO, K1, YO, *P3tog, YO, K1, YO; rep from * to last 2 sts, P2tog.

Rep these 2 rows for patt.

Making a Block

To make Small (Large) block with border:

CO 30 (46) sts.

Knit 5 (9) rows.

Dec row: K5 (8), K2tog, [K7 (12), K2tog] twice, K5 (8)—27 (43) sts.

Keeping first and last 3 (5) sts in garter st, work rows 1 and 2 of Lacy Openwork patt over rem sts.

Rep rows 1 and 2 another 17 (29) times for a total of 36 (60) patt rows.

Inc row: K5 (7), M1, [K8 (14), M1] twice, K6 (8)—30 (46) sts.

Knit 5 (9) rows.

BO kw on RS.

Bluebell Rib

Stitch Pattern

Multiple of 5 sts + 2 sts

Rows 1 and 3 (RS): P2, *K3, P2; rep from * to end.

Rows 2 and 4: K2, *P3, K2; rep from * to end.

Row 5: P2, *YO, sl 1, K2tog, psso, YO, P2; rep from * to end.

Row 6: K2, *P3, K2; rep from * to end.

Rep these 6 rows for patt.

Making a Block

To make Small (Large) block with border:

CO 30 (46) sts.

Knit 5 (9) rows.

Dec row: K3 (5), *K5 (3), K2tog, K5 (4); rep from * to last 3 (5) sts, K3 (5)—28 (42) sts.

Keeping first and last 3 (5) sts in garter st, work rows 1–6 of Bluebell Rib patt over rem sts.

Rep rows 1–6 another 5 (9) times for a total of 36 (60) patt rows.

Inc row: K3 (5), *K5 (4), M1, K6 (4); rep from * to last 3 (5) sts, K3 (5)—30 (46) sts.

Knit 5 (9) rows.

BO kw on RS.

Waterfall

Stitch Pattern

Multiple of 6 sts + 3 sts

Row 1 (RS): P3, *K3, YO, P3; rep from * to end.

Row 2: K3, *P4, K3; rep from * to end.

Row 3: P3, *K1, K2tog, YO, K1, P3; rep from * to end.

Row 4: K3, *P2, P2tog, K3; rep from * to end.

Row 5: P3, *K1, YO, K2tog, P3; rep from * to end.

Row 6: K3, *P3, K3; rep from * to end.

Rep these 6 rows for patt.

Making a Block

To make Small (Large) block with border:

CO 30 (46) sts.

Knit 5 (9) rows.

Dec row: K6 (10), K2tog, K6 (10), K2tog, K6 (10), K2tog, K6 (10)—27 (43) sts.

Keeping first and last 3 (5) sts in garter st, work rows 1–6 of Waterfall patt over rem sts.

Rep rows 1–6 another 5 (9) times for a total of 36 (60) patt rows.

Inc row: K7 (11), M1, K7 (11), M1, K7 (11), M1, K6 (10)—30 (46) sts.

Knit 5 (9) rows.

BO kw on RS.

Double-Eyelet Rib

Stitch Pattern

Multiple of 7 sts + 2 sts

Row 1 (RS): P2, *K5, P2; rep from * to end.

Row 2: K2, *P5, K2; rep from * to end.

Row 3: P2, *K2tog, YO, K1, YO, sl 1, K1, psso, P2; rep from * to end.

Row 4: Rep row 2.

Rep these 4 rows for patt.

Making a Block

To make Small (Large) block with border:

CO 30 (46) sts.

Knit 5 (9) rows.

Dec/inc row: K14 (23), K2tog (M1), K14 (23)—29 (47) sts.

Keeping first and last 3 (5) sts in garter st, work rows 1–4 of Double-Eyelet Rib patt over rem sts.

Rep rows 1–4 another 8 (14) times for a total of 36 (60) patt rows.

Inc/dec row: K15 (23), M1 (K2tog), K14 (22)—30 (46) sts.

Knit 5 (9) rows.

BO kw on RS.

Little Shell Pattern

Stitch Pattern

Multiple of 7 sts + 2 sts

Row 1 (RS): Knit.

Row 2: Purl.

Row 3: K2, *YO, P1, P3tog, P1, YO, K2; rep from * to end.

Row 4: Purl.

Rep these 4 rows for patt.

Making a Block

To make Small (Large) block with border:

CO 30 (46) sts.

Knit 5 (9) rows.

Inc row: K14 (23), K2tog (M1), K14 (23)—29 (47) sts.

Keeping first and last 3 (5) sts in garter st, work rows 1–4 of Little Shell Pattern over rem sts.

Rep rows 1–4 another 8 (14) times for a total of 36 (60) patt rows.

Next row: K15 (23), M1 (K2tog), K14 (22)—30 (46) sts.

Knit 5 (9) rows.

BO kw on RS.

Fishtail Lace Panel

Stitch Pattern

Worked over 11 sts on a background of St st

Row 1 (RS): P1, K1, YO, K2, sl 1, K2tog, psso, K2, YO, K1, P1.

Rows 2 and 4: K1, P9, K1.

Row 3: P1, K2, YO, K1, sl 1, K2tog, psso, K1, YO, K2, P1.

Row 5: P1, K3, YO, sl 1, K2tog, psso, YO, K3, P1.

Row 6: Rep row 2.

Rep these 6 rows for patt.

Making a Block

To make Small (Large) block with border:

CO 30 (46) sts.

Knit 6 (10) rows.

Keeping first and last 3 (5) sts in garter st, work Fishtail Lace Panel patt over rem sts as follows:

Row 1 (RS): K1, *work row 1 of Fishtail Lace Panel patt; rep from * to last 1 (2) st, K1 (2).

Row 2: P1 (2), *work row 2 of Fishtail Lace Panel; rep from * to last st, P1.

Row 3: K1, *work row 3 of Fishtail Lace Panel; rep from * to last 1 (2) st, K1 (2).

Row 4: P1 (2), *work row 4 of Fishtail Lace Panel; rep from * to last st, P1.

Row 5: K1, *work row 5 of Fishtail Lace Panel; rep from * to last 1 (2) st, K1 (2).

Row 6: P1 (2), *work row 6 of Fishtail Lace Panel; rep from * to last st, P1.

Rep rows 1–6 another 5 (9) times for a total of 36 (60) patt rows.

Knit 6 (10) rows.

BO kw on RS.

Diamond Panel

Stitch Pattern

*Worked over 11 sts on a background of reverse
St st*

Row 1 (RS): P2, K2tog, (K1, YO) twice, K1, sl 1, K1,
psso, P2.

Row 2 and all even-numbered rows: K2, P7, K2.

Row 3: P2, K2tog, YO, K3, YO, sl 1, K1, psso, P2.

Row 5: P2, K1, YO, sl 1, K1, psso, K1, K2tog, YO,
K1, P2.

Row 7: P2, K2, YO, sl 1, K2tog, psso, YO, K2, P2.

Row 8: Rep row 2.

Rep these 8 rows for patt.

Making a Block

To make Small (Large) block with border:

CO 30 (46) sts.

Knit 6 (10) rows.

Keeping first and last 3 (5) sts in garter st, work
Diamond Panel patt over rem sts as follows:

Row 1 (RS): K0 (5), *work row 1 of Diamond Panel
patt**, K2 (4); rep from * to ** one time, K0 (5).

Row 2 and all even-numbered rows: P0 (5), *work
row 2 of Diamond Panel**, P2 (4); rep from * to **
one time, P0 (5).

Row 3: K0 (5), * work row 3 of Diamond Panel **,
K2 (4); rep from * to ** one time, K0 (5).

Row 5: K0 (5), *work row 5 of Diamond Panel**,
K2 (4); rep from * to ** one time, K0 (5).

Row 7: K0 (5), *work row 7 of Diamond Panel **,
K2 (4); rep from * to ** one time, K0 (5).

Row 8: Rep row 2.

Rep rows 1–8 another 3 (6) times and then work
rows 1–5 once more.

Knit 5 (9) rows.

BO kw on RS.

Little Fountain Pattern

Stitch Pattern

Multiple of 4 sts + 1 st

Row 1 (RS): K1, *YO, K3, YO, K1; rep from * to end.

Row 2: Purl.

Row 3: K2, sl 1, K2tog, psso, *K3, sl 1, K2tog, psso; rep from * to last 2 sts, K2.

Row 4: Rep row 2.

Rep these 4 rows for patt.

Making a Block

To make Small (Large) block with border:

CO 30 (46) sts.

Knit 5 (9) rows.

Dec row: [K6 (10), K2tog] 3 times, K6 (10)— 27 (43) sts.

Keeping first and last 3 (5) sts in garter st, work rows 1–4 of Little Fountain Pattern over rem sts.

Rep rows 1–4 another 8 (14) times for a total of 36 (60) patt rows.

Inc row: K6 (11), M1, [K7 (11), M1] twice; K7 (10)— 30 (46) sts.

Knit 5 (9) rows.

BO kw on RS.

Faggoting

Stitch Pattern

Multiple of 3 sts

Row 1 (RS): *K1, YO twice, K2tog; rep from * to end.

Row 2: P1, *purl into first YO of previous row, drop 2nd YO off needle, P2; rep from * to last 3 sts, purl into first YO, drop 2nd YO off needle, P1.

Row 3: *K2tog, YO twice, K1; rep from * to end.

Row 4: Rep row 2.

Rep these 4 rows for patt.

Making a Block

To make Small (Large) block with border:

CO 30 (46) sts.

Knit 5 (9) rows.

Dec row: K4 (7), K2tog, [K2 (4), K2tog] 5 times, K4 (7)—24 (40) sts.

Keeping first and last 3 (5) sts in garter st, work rows 1–4 of Faggoting patt over rem sts.

Rep rows 1–4 another 8 (14) times for a total of 36 (60) patt rows.

Inc row: K5 (8), M1, [K3 (5), M1] 5 times, K4 (7)— 30 (46) sts.

Knit 5 (9) rows.

BO kw on RS.

Feather Rib

Stitch Pattern

Multiple of 5 sts + 2 sts

Row 1 (RS): P2, *YO, K2tog tbl, K1, P2; rep from * to end.

Row 2: K2, *YO, K2tog tbl, P1, K2; rep from * to end.

Rep these 2 rows for patt.

Making a Block

To make Small (Large) block with border:

CO 30 (46) sts.

Knit 5 (9) rows.

Dec row (WS): K9 (6), K2tog, *K8 (6), K2tog; rep from * to last 9 (6) sts, K9 (6)—28 (42) sts.

Keeping first and last 3 (5) sts in garter st, work rows 1 and 2 of Feather Rib patt over rem sts.

Rep rows 1 and 2 another 17 (29) times for a total of 36 (60) patt rows.

Inc row (RS): K10 (7), M1, *K9 (7), M1; rep from * to last 9 (6) sts, K9 (6)—30 (46) sts.

Knit 5 (9) rows.

BO kw on RS.

Lacy Checks

Stitch Pattern

Multiple of 6 sts + 5 sts

Rows 1 and 3 (RS): K1, *YO, sl 1, K2tog, psso, YO, K3; rep from * to last 4 sts, YO, sl 1, K2tog, psso, YO, K1.

Row 2 and all even-numbered rows: Purl.

Row 5: Knit.

Rows 7 and 9: K4, *YO, sl 1, K2tog, psso, YO, K3; rep from * to last st, K1.

Row 11: Knit.

Row 12: Purl.

Rep these 12 rows for patt.

Making a Block

To make Small (Large) block with border:

CO 30 (46) sts.

Knit 5 (9) rows.

Dec row: K14 (22), K2tog, K14 (22)—29 (45) sts.

Keeping first and last 3 (5) sts in garter st, work rows 1–12 of Lacy Checks patt over rem sts.

Rep rows 1–12 another 2 (4) times for a total of 36 (60) patt rows.

Inc row: K14 (22), M1, K15 (23)—30 (46) sts.

Knit 5 (9) rows.

BO kw on RS.

Mock Cable—Right

Stitch Pattern

Multiple of 4 sts + 2 sts

Row 1 (RS): P2, *K2, P2; rep from * to end.

Row 2: K2, *P2, K2; rep from * to end.

Row 3: P2, *cross 2 front, P2; rep from * to end.

Row 4: Rep row 2.

Rep these 4 rows for patt.

Making a Block

To make Small (Large) block with border:

CO 30 (46) sts.

K5 (9) rows.

Inc row (RS): K12 (8), *M1, K6; rep from * to last 12 (8) sts, M1, K12 (8)—32 (52) sts.

Keeping first and last 3 (5) sts in garter st, work rows 1–4 of Mock Cable—Right patt over rem sts.

Rep rows 1–4 another 8 (14) times for a total of 36 (60) patt rows.

Dec row (RS): K11 (7), K2tog, *K5, K2tog; rep from * to last 12 (8) sts, K12 (8)—30 (46) sts.

Knit 5 (9) rows.

BO kw on RS.

Little Hourglass Rib

Stitch Pattern

Multiple of 4 sts + 2 sts

Row 1 (WS): K2, *P2, K2; rep from * to end.

Row 2 (RS): P2, *K2tog tbl, then knit same 2 sts tog through front loops, P2; rep from * to end.

Row 3: K2, *P1, YO, P1, K2; rep from * to end.

Row 4: P2, *sl 1 wyib, K1, psso, K1, P2; rep from * to end.

Rep these 4 rows for patt.

Making a Block

To make Small (Large) block with border:

CO 30 (46) sts.

Knit 5 (9) rows.

Inc row (WS): K12 (8), M1, [K6, M1] 1 (5) time, K12 (8)—32 (52) sts.

Set-up row (RS): K3 (5), P2, *K2, P2; rep from * to last 3 (5) sts, K3 (5).

Keeping first and last 3 (5) sts in garter st, work rows 1–4 of Little Hourglass Rib patt over rem sts.

Rep rows 1–4 another 7 (13) times and then work rows 1–3 once more.

Dec row (RS): K11 (7), K2tog, [K5, K2tog] 1 (5) time, K12 (8)—30 (46) sts.

Knit 5 (9) more rows.

BO kw on RS.

Mock-Cable Rib

Stitch Pattern

Multiple of 7 sts + 2 sts

Row 1 (RS): P2, *cross 2 back, K3, P2; rep from *
to end.

Row 2 and all even-numbered rows: K2, *P5, K2;
rep from * to end.

Row 3: P2, *K1, cross 2 back, K2, P2; rep from *
to end.

Row 5: P2, *K2, cross 2 back, K1, P2; rep from *
to end.

Row 7: P2, *K3, cross 2 back, P2; rep from * to end.

Row 8: K2, *P5, K2; rep from * to end.

Rep these 8 rows for patt.

Making a Block

To make Small (Large) block with border:

CO 30 (46) stitches.

Knit 5 (9) rows.

Inc/dec row: K14 (23), K2tog (M1), K14 (23)—
29 (47) sts.

Set-up row 1 (RS): K3 (5); P2, *K5, P2; rep from * to
last 3 (5) sts, K3 (5).

Set-up row 2: K5 (7); *P5, K2; rep from * to last
3 (5) sts, K3 (5).

Keeping first and last 3 (5) sts in garter st, work rows
1–8 of Mock-Cable Rib patt over rem sts.

Rep rows 1–8 another 3 (6) times and then work
set-up rows 1 and 2 once more.

Inc/dec row: K15 (23), M1 (K2tog), K14 (22)—
30 (46) sts.

Knit 5 (9) rows.

BO kw on RS.

Eyelet Mock-Cable Rib

Stitch Pattern

Multiple of 5 sts + 2 sts

Row 1 (RS): P2, *sl 1, K2, psso, P2; rep from * to end.

Row 2: K2, *P1, YO, P1, K2; rep from * to end.

Row 3: P2, *K3, P2; rep from * to end.

Row 4: K2, *P3, K2; rep from * to end.

Rep these 4 rows for patt.

Making a Block

To make Small (Large) block with border:

CO 30 (46) sts.

Knit 5 (9) rows.

Dec row: K9 (7), K2tog, *K8, K2tog; rep from * to last 9 (7) sts, K9 (7)—28 (42) sts.

Keeping first and last 3 (5) sts in garter st, work rows 1–4 of Eyelet Mock-Cable Rib patt over rem sts.

Rep rows 1–4 another 8 (14) times for a total of 36 (60) patt rows.

Work row 1 once more.

Inc row: K9 (10), M1, *K11, M1; rep from * to last 8 (10) sts, K8 (K5, M1, K5)—30 (46) sts.

Knit 4 (8) rows.

BO kw on RS.

Allover Lattice Stitch

Stitch Pattern

Multiple of 12 sts + 2 sts

Row 1 and all WS rows: Purl.

Row 2 (RS): Knit.

Row 4: K1, *C4B, K4, C4F; rep from * to last st, K1.

Row 6: Knit.

Row 8: K3, C4F, C4B, *K4, C4F, C4B; rep from * to last 3 sts, K3.

Rep these 8 rows for patt.

Making a Block

To make Small (Large) block with border:

CO 30 (46) sts.

K5 (9) rows.

Inc row: K9 (17), M1, K12, M1, K9 (17)—32 (48) sts.

Next row: Knit.

Keeping first and last 3 (5) sts in garter st, work rows 1–8 of Allover Lattice Stitch patt over rem sts.

Rep rows 1–8 another 3 (6) times and then work rows 1–3 once more.

Dec row: K4 (7), *C4B, K1, K2tog, K1, C4F; rep from * to last 4 (6) sts, K4 (6)—30 (46) sts.

K5 (9) rows.

BO kw on RS.

Claw Pattern 1

Stitch Pattern

Worked over 8 sts on a background of reverse St st

Row 1 (RS): Knit.

Rows 2 and 4: Purl.

Row 3: C4B, C4F.

Rep these 4 rows for patt.

Making a Block

To make Small (Large) block with border:

CO 30 (46) sts.

Knit 5 (9) rows.

Inc row: K9 (10), [M1, K2, M1, K6] 2 (4) times,
    K5 (4)—34 (54) sts.

Keeping first and last 3 (5) sts in garter st, work patt
    as follows:

Row 1 (RS): P0 (1), *P3, work row 1 of Claw Pattern
    1, P3; rep from * to last 0 (1) st, P0 (1).

Row 2: K0 (1), *K3, work row 2 of Claw Pattern 1,
    K3; rep from * to last 0 (1) st, K0 (1).

Row 3: P0 (1), *P3, work row 3 of Claw Pattern 1, P3;
    rep from * to last 0 (1) st, P0 (1).

Row 4: K0 (1), *K3, work row 4 of Claw Pattern 1,
    K3; rep from * to last 0 (1) st, K0 (1).

Rep rows 1–4 another 8 (14) times for a total of
    36 (60) patt rows.

Dec row: K9 (10), [K2tog twice, K6] 2 (4) times,
    K5 (4)—30 (46) sts.

Knit 5 (9) rows.

BO kw on RS.

Forked Cable

Stitch Pattern

Multiple of 8 sts + 2 sts

Rows 1, 3, 5, and 7 (WS): Purl.

Rows 2, 4, and 6 (RS): P3, K4, *P4, K4; rep from * to
    last 3 sts, P3.

Row 8: K3, P4, *K4, P4; rep from * to last 3 sts, K3.

Row 9: Purl.

Row 10: K1, *C4F, C4B; rep from * to last st, K1.

Rep these 10 rows for patt.

Making a Block

To make Small (Large) block with border:

CO 30 (46) sts.

Knit 6 (10) rows.

Inc row (RS): K12 (8), M1, *K6, M1; rep from * to last
    12 (8) sts, M1, K12 (8)—32 (52) sts.

Keeping first and last 3 (5) sts in garter st, work rows
    1–10 of Forked Cable patt over rem sts.

Rep rows 1–10 of Forked Cable patt another 2 (4)
    times and then work rows 1–5 (1–9) once more.

Dec row (RS): K11 (7), K2tog, *K5, K2tog; rep from *
    to last 12 (8) sts, K12 (8)—30 (46) sts.

Knit 5 (9) rows.

BO kw on RS.

Double Cable

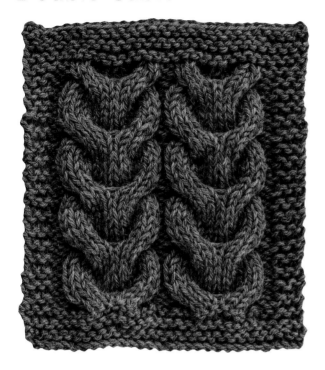

Stitch Pattern

Worked over 12 sts on a background of reverse St st

Note: This pattern can be worked so cable goes downward instead of upward; the only difference is in row 3 of stitch pattern (see below.)

Rows 1, 5, and 7 (RS): Knit.

Row 2 and all even-numbered rows: Purl.

Row 3: C6B, C6F for upward cable *OR* C6F, C6B for downward cable

Row 8: Purl.

Rep these 8 rows for patt.

Making a Block

To make Small (Large) block with border:

CO 30 (46) sts.

Knit 5 (9) rows.

Inc row: K6 (12), M1, (K4, M1) twice, K2 (6), M1, (K4, M1) twice, K6 (12)—36 (52) sts.

Keeping first and last 3 (5) sts in garter st, work Double Cable patt over rem sts.

Row 1 (RS): P2 (6), work row 1 of Double Cable patt, P2 (6), work row 1 of Double Cable patt, P2 (6).

Row 2: K2 (6), work row 2 of Double Cable patt, K2 (6), work row 2 of Double Cable patt, K2 (6).

Row 3: P2 (6), work row 3 of Double Cable patt, P2 (6), work row 3 of Double Cable patt, P2 (6).

Row 4: Rep row 2.

Rows 5 and 7: Rep row 1.

Rows 6 and 8: Rep row 2.

Rep rows 1–8 another 3 (6) times and then work rows 1–4 once more for a total of 36 (60) patt rows.

Dec row: K6 (12), K2tog, (K2, K2tog) twice, K4 (8), K2tog, (K2, K2tog) twice, K6 (12)—30 (46) sts.

Knit 5 (9) rows.

BO kw on RS.

Staghorn Cable 2

Stitch Pattern

Worked over 16 sts on a background of reverse St st

Row 1 (RS): C4F, K8, C4B.

Rows 2 and 4: Purl.

Row 3: K2, C4F, K4, C4B, K2.

Row 5: K4, C4F, C4B, K4.

Row 6: Purl.

Rep these 6 rows for patt.

Making a Block

To make Small (Large) block with border:

CO 30 (46) sts.

Knit 6 (10) rows.

Set-up row 1 (RS): K3 (5), P6 (4); *M1, K4, M1, K4, M1, K4, M1**, P0 (4); rep from * to ** 0 (1) time, P6 (4), K3 (5)—34 (54) sts.

Set-up row 2: K9, P16, K0 (4), P0 (16), K9.

Keeping first and last 3 (5) sts in garter st, work patt as follows:

Row 1 (RS): P6 (4), *work row 1 of Staghorn Cable 2 patt over next 16 sts**, P0 (4); rep from * to ** 0 (1) time, P6 (4).

Rows 2, 4, and 6: K6 (4), P16 for next row of Staghorn Cable 2 patt, K0 (4), P0 (16) for next row of Staghorn Cable 2 patt, K6 (4).

Row 3: P6 (4), *work row 3 of Staghorn Cable 2 patt over next 16 sts**, P0 (4); rep from * to ** 0 (1) time, P6 (4).

Row 5: P6 (4), *work row 5 of Staghorn Cable 2 patt over next 16 sts**, P0 (4); rep from * to ** 0 (1) time, P6 (4).

Rep rows 1–6 another 4 (8) times and then work rows 1 and 2 once more.

Dec row (RS): K3 (5), P6 (4), *ssk, C4F, K2tog, ssk, C4B, K2tog**, P0 (4); rep from * to ** 0 (1) time, P6 (4), K3 (5)—30 (46) sts.

Next row: K9, P12, K0 (4), P0 (16), K9.

Knit 6 (10) rows.

BO kw on RS.

Eight-Stitch Cable

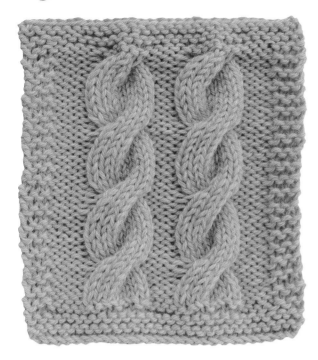

Stitch Pattern

Worked over 8 sts on a background of reverse St st

Note: This pattern can be worked with a left- or right-slanting cable; the only difference is how you cross the cables on row 5.

Row 1 (RS): Knit.

Row 2: Purl.

Rows 3 and 4: Rep rows 1 and 2.

Row 5: C8B for right-twist cable *OR* C8F for left-twist cable.

Row 6: Purl.

Rows 7–10: Rep rows 1 and 2 twice more.

Rep these 10 rows for patt.

Making a Block

To make Small (Large) block with border:

CO 30 (46) sts.

Knit 6 (10) rows.

Set-up row 1 (RS): K3 (5), P4 (5), *K2, M1, K2, M1, K2, P4; rep from * to last 3 (6) sts, P0 (1), K3 (5)—34 (52) sts.

Set-up row 2 (WS): K7 (10), *P8, K4; rep from * to last 3 (6) sts, K3 (6).

Keeping first and last 3 (5) sts in garter stitch, work Eight-Stitch Cable patt over rem sts as follows:

Row 1: P4 (5), *work row 1 of Eight-Stitch Cable patt over next 8 sts, P4; rep from * to last 0 (1) st, P0 (1).

Row 2: K4 (5), *work row 2 of Eight-Stitch Cable patt over next 8 sts, K4; rep from * to last 0 (1) st, K0 (1).

Row 3: P4 (5), *work row 3 of Eight-Stitch Cable patt over next 8 sts, P4; rep from * to last 0 (1) st, P1.

Row 4: K4 (5), *work row 4 of Eight-Stitch Cable patt over next 8 sts, K4; rep from * to last 0 (1) st, K1.

Row 5: P4 (5), *work row 5 of Eight-Stitch Cable patt over next 8 sts, P4; rep from * to last 0 (1) st, P1.

Row 6: K4 (5), *work row 6 of Eight-Stitch Cable patt over next 8 sts, K4; rep from * to last 0 (1) st, K1.

Row 7: P4 (5), *work row 7 of Eight-Stitch Cable patt over next 8 sts, P4; rep from * to last 0 (1) st, P1.

Row 8: K4 (5), *work row 8 of Eight-Stitch Cable patt over next 8 sts, K4; rep from * to last 0 (1) st, K1.

Row 9: P4 (5), *work row 9 of Eight-Stitch Cable patt over next 8 sts, P4; rep from * to last 0 (1) st, P1.

Row 10: K4 (5), *work row 10 of Eight-Stitch Cable patt over next 8 sts, K4; rep from * to last 0 (1) st, K1.

Rep rows 1–10 another 2 (4) times and then work rows 1–4 (1–8) once more.

Dec row: K3 (5), P4 (5), *slip next 4 sts to cable needle and hold in back of work, K1, K2tog, K1, bring cable needle back to front and work those sts as follows: K1, K2tog, K1, P4; rep from * to last 3 (6) sts, P0 (1), K3 (5)—30 (46) sts.

Knit 5 (9) rows.

BO kw on RS.

Knotted Cable

Stitch Pattern

Worked over 6 sts on a background of reverse St st

Row 1 (RS): K2, P2, K2.

Row 2 and all even-numbered rows: P2, K2, P2.

Row 3: Cross 6.

Rows 5, 7, and 9: Rep row 1.

Row 10: Rep row 2.

Rep these 10 rows for patt.

Making a Block

To make Small (Large) block with border:

CO 30 (46) sts.

Knit 6 (10) rows.

Set-up row 1: K3 (5), P5 (7), *K1, M1, P2, M1, K1, P5; rep from * to last 4 (7) sts, P1 (2), K3 (5)— 34 (52) sts.

Set-up row 2: K9 (12), *P2, K2, P2, K5; rep from * to last 3 (7) sts, K3 (7).

Keeping first and last 3 (5) sts in garter st, work as follows over rem sts:

Row 1 (RS): P5 (7), *work row 1 of Knotted Cable patt over next 6 sts, P5; rep from * 1 (2) more time, P1 (2).

Row 2: K6 (7), *work row 2 of Knotted Cable patt over next 6 sts, K5; rep from * 1 (2) more time, K0 (2).

Row 3: P5 (7), *work row 3 of Knotted Cable patt over next 6 sts, P5; rep from * 1 (2) more time, P1 (2).

Row 4: K6 (7), *work row 4 of Knotted Cable patt over next 6 sts, K5; rep from * 1 (2) more time, K0 (2).

Row 5: P5 (7), *work row 5 of Knotted Cable patt over next 6 sts, P5; rep from * 1 (2) more time, P1 (2).

Row 6: K6 (7), *work row 6 of Knotted Cable patt over next 6 sts, K5; rep from * 1 (2) more time, K0 (2).

Row 7: P5 (7), *work row 7 of Knotted Cable patt over next 6 sts, P5; rep from * 1 (2) more time, P1 (2).

Row 8: K6 (7), *work row 8 of Knotted Cable patt over next 6 sts, K5; rep from * 1 (2) more time, K0 (2).

Row 9: P5 (7), *work row 9 of Knotted Cable patt over next 6 sts, P5; rep from * 1 (2) more time, P1 (2).

Row 10: K6 (7), *work row 10 of Knotted Cable patt over next 6 sts, K5; rep from * 1 (2) more time, K0 (2).

Rep rows 1–10 another 2 (4) times and then work rows 1–4 (1–8) once more.

Dec row (RS): K3 (5), P5 (7), *K2tog, P2, K2tog, P5; rep from * to last 4 (7) sts; P1 (2), K3 (5)— 30 (46) sts.

Knit 5 (9) rows.

BO kw on RS.

Braided Cable

Stitch Pattern

Worked over 9 sts on a background of reverse St st

Row 1: T3F, T3B, T3F.

Row 2: P2, K2, P4, K1.

Row 3: P1, C4B, P2, K2.

Row 4: Rep row 2.

Row 5: T3B, T3F, T3B.

Row 6: K1, P4, K2, P2.

Row 7: K2, P2, C4F, P1.

Row 8: Rep row 6.

Rep these 8 rows for patt.

Making a Block

To make Small (Large) block with border:

CO 30 (46) sts.

Knit 5 (9) rows.

Inc row (WS): K7 (9),*M1, K4, M1**, K9 (10), M1, K4, M1, K3 (7); rep from * to ** 0 (1) time, K3 (8)—34 (52) sts.

Keeping first and last 3 (5) sts in garter st, work as follows over rem sts:

Row 1 (RS): *P3, work row 1 of Braided Cable patt over next 9 sts, P1; rep from * 1 (2) more time, P2 (3).

Row 2: *K3 (4), work row 2 of Braided Cable patt over next 9 sts, K1 (0); rep from * 1 (2) more time, K2 (3).

Row 3: *P3, work row 3 of Braided Cable patt over next 9 sts, P1; rep from * 1 (2) more time, P2 (3).

Row 4: *K3 (4), work row 4 of Braided Cable patt over next 9 sts, K1 (0); rep from * 1 (2) more time, K2 (3).

Row 5: *P3, work row 5 of Braided Cable patt over next 9 sts, P1; rep from * 1 (2) more time, P2 (3).

Row 6: *K3 (4), work row 6 of Braided Cable patt over next 9 sts, K1 (0); rep from * 1 (2) more time, K2 (3).

Row 7: *P3, work row 7 of Braided Cable patt over next 9 sts, P1; rep from * 1 (2) more time, P2 (3).

Row 8: *K3 (4), work row 6 of Braided Cable patt over next 9 sts, K1 (0); rep from * 1 (2) more time, K2 (3).

Rep rows 1–8 another 3 (6) times and then rows 1–4 once more for a total of 36 (60) patt rows.

Dec row: K6 (9), *K2tog, K5, K2tog**, K4 (5), K2tog, K5, K2tog, K3 (6); rep from * to ** 0 (1) times, K3 (5)—30 (46) sts.

Knit 5 (9) rows.

BO kw on RS.

Nine-Stitch Braid—Upward

Stitch Pattern

Worked over 9 sts on a background of reverse St st

Row 1 (RS): Knit.

Row 2 and all even-numbered rows: Purl.

Row 3: C6B, K3.

Row 5: Knit.

Row 7: K3, C6F.

Row 8: Purl.

Rep these 8 rows for patt.

Making a Block

To make Small (Large) block with border:

CO 30 (46) sts.

Knit 5 (9) rows.

Inc row: K8 (13), *M1, K3, M1, K6; rep from * to last 4 (6) sts, K4 (6)—34 (52) sts.

Inc row (Small only): (K6, M1) 4 times, K6—34 sts.

Inc row (Large only): (K8, M1) 5 times, K6—51 sts.

Keeping first and last 3 (5) sts in garter st, work as follows over rem sts:

Row 1 (RS): P3, work row 1 of Nine-Stitch Braid patt over next 9 sts, *P4, work row 1 of Nine-Stitch Braid over next 9 sts; rep from * to last 3 (4) sts, P3 (4).

Row 2: K3 (4), work row 2 of Braid, *K4, work row 2 of Braid patt; rep from * to last 3 sts, K3.

Row 3: P3, work row 3 of Braid, *P4, work row 3 of Braid patt; rep from * to last 3 (4) sts, P3 (4).

Row 4: K3 (4), work row 4 of Braid, *K4, work row 4 of Braid patt; rep from * to last 3 sts, K3.

Row 5: P3, work row 5 of Braid, *P4, work row 5 of Braid patt; rep from * to last 3 (4) sts, P3 (4).

Row 6: K3, work row 6 of Braid, *K4, work row 6 of Braid patt; rep from * to last 3 sts, K3.

Row 7: P3, work row 7 of Braid, *P4, work row 7 of Braid patt; rep from * to last 3 sts, P3.

Row 8: K3, work row 8 of Braid, *K4, work row 8 of Braid patt; rep from 8 to last 3 sts, K3.

Rep rows 1–8 another 3 (6) times and then work rows 1–4 once more for a total of 36 (60) patt rows.

Dec row (Small only): K6, (K2tog, K5) 4 times—30 sts.

Dec row (Large only): K6, (K2tog, K7) 5 times—46 sts.

Knit 5(9) rows.

BO kw on RS.

Garter and Stockinette Cable

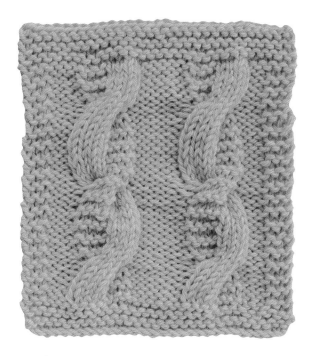

Stitch Pattern

Worked over 8 sts on a background of reverse St st

Rows 1, 3, and 5 (RS): Knit.

Rows 2, 4, and 6: P4, K4.

Row 7: C8B.

Rows 8, 10, 12, 14, 16, and 18: K4, P4.

Rows 9, 11, 13, 15, and 17: Knit.

Row 19: C8B.

Rows 20 and 22: P4, K4.

Rows 21 and 23: Knit.

Row 24: P4, K4.

Rep these 24 rows for patt.

Making a Block

To make Small (Large) block with border:

CO 30 (46) sts.

Knit 5 (9) rows.

Inc row: K7 (13), M1, K4, M1, K9 (12), M1, K4, M1, K6 (13)—34 (50) sts.

Keeping first and last 3 (5) sts in garter st, work patt as follows:

Row 1 (RS): P3 (8), work row 1 of Garter and Stockinette Cable patt, P6 (8), work row 1 of Garter and Stockinette Cable patt, P3 (8).

Row 2: K3 (8), work row 2 of Garter and Stockinette Cable patt, K6 (8), work row 2 of Garter and Stockinette Cable patt, K3 (8).

Row 3: P3 (8), work row 3 of Garter and Stockinette Cable patt, P6 (8); work row 3 of Garter and Stockinette Cable patt, P3 (8).

Row 4: K3 (8), work row 4 of Garter and Stockinette Cable patt, K6 (8), work row 4 of Garter and Stockinette Cable patt, K3 (8).

Continue to work rows 5–24 of patt as established.

Rep rows 1–12 (1–24) one more time and then work rows (1–12) another 0 (1) time for a total of 36 (60) patt rows.

Dec row: K6 (12), K2tog, K4, K2tog, K6 (10), K2tog, K4, K2tog, K6 (12)—30 (46) sts.

Knit 5 (9) rows.

BO kw on RS.

Four-Stitch Cable 2

Stitch Pattern

Done on a background of reverse St st

Row 1 (RS): Knit.

Row 2: Purl.

Row 3: Cable 4 back.

Row 4: Purl.

Rep these four rows for patt.

Note: These instructions result in a cable that twists to the right. To twist the cable to the left, you would want to replace the "Cable 4 back" in row 3 with a "Cable 4 front."

Making a Block

To make Small (Large) block with border:

CO 30 (46) sts.

Knit 5 (9) rows.

Inc Row: K3 (5); *K6, M1, K6; rep from * to last 3 (5) sts; K3 (5)—32 (49) sts.

Keeping first and last 3 (5) sts in garter st, work rows 1-4 of Four-Stitch Cable 2 patt over rem sts as follows:

Row 1 (RS): *P5 (4), work row 1 of Cable patt, P3 (5); rep from * to last 2 (0) sts; P2 (0).

Row 2: *K5 (5), work row 2 of Cable patt, K3 (5); rep from * to last 5 (4) sts; P5 (4).

Row 3: *P5 (4), work row 3 of Cable patt, P3 (5); rep from * to last 2 (0) sts; P2 (0).

Row 4: *5 (5), work row 2 of Cable patt, K3 (5); rep fom * to last 5 (4) sts; P5 (4).

Rep Rows 1-4 another 8 (14) times for a total of 36 (60) pattern rows.

Dec row: K3 (5); *K5, K2tog, K6; rep from * to last 3 (5) sts; K3 (5)—30 (46) sts.

K5 (9) rows.

BO kw on RS.

Sampler-Type
Afghans

Small-Blocks Sampler Afghan

This is a great afghan to make while learning different stitch patterns. Use the 64 stitch patterns I chose, or pick your own for a delightfully one-of-a-kind afghan.

"Small-Blocks Sampler Afghan," designed and made by author

Skill Level

Easy ■■□□ to Experienced ■■■■ ,
depending on the blocks chosen

Size

Approx 50" x 58" blocked; each block measures
approx 6" x 7" blocked

Materials

Yarn: Cascade 220 by Cascade Yarns (100% wool;
100 g; 220 yds) OR an equivalent worsted-weight
yarn (■4■)

- **A** 3 skeins of color 2444 (Flame) *OR* approx
  500 yds
- **B** 3 skeins of color 2436 (Mimosa) *OR* approx
  500 yds
- **C** 3 skeins of color 9455 (Turquoise Heather) *OR*
  approx 500 yds
- **D** 3 skeins of color 9322 (Silver Spruce Heather)
  OR approx 500 yds
- **E** 3 skeins of color 9457 (Cobalt Heather) *OR*
  approx 500 yds
- **F** 2 skeins of color 2450 (Mystic Purple) *OR*
  approx 400 yds

Needles: Size 7 (4.5 mm) needles *OR* size needed
to attain gauge; size G crochet hook for border

Gauge

20 sts and 28 rows = 4" in St st

Instructions

Make 64 small blocks. Choose pattern stitches
of your own or follow the chart on page 62 if you
choose to make the same blocks as in the sample
shown.

Doreen's Hint

You can leave longer tails at both the cast-on
and bind-off edges and use these for at least
some of the seaming.

Finishing

Block each individual block to size. Lay out blocks
in sequence shown in chart. Seam together cast-
on/bind-off edges of blocks using cast-on edge
to bind-off edge assembly method (page 91) so
that you will have 8 columns of blocks. Seam each
column to next column using garter-stitch assembly
method (page 91).

Outer Border

Work border of your choice around entire outside
edge of afghan using color of your choosing. The
sample shown has a backward crochet edging.
  Weave in ends.

Small-Blocks Sampler Afghan—Block Placement

Garter-Stitch Steps Page 18	Embossed Check Stitch Page 22	Tile Stitch Page 17	Bobble Rib Page 40	Broken-Rib Diagonal Page 21	Ridged Lace 1 Page 27	Sailors' Rib Page 21	Lacy Checks Page 46
Farrow Rib Page 16	Diagonal Seed Stitch Page 12	Feather Rib Page 46	Garter-Stitch Ridges Page 11	Nine-Stitch Braid— Upward Page 56	Broken Rib Page 15	Bamboo Stitch Page 29	Little Hourglass Rib Page 47
Corded Rib Page 33	Forked Cable Page 50	Crocus Buds Page 29	Fleck Stitch Page 13	Faggoting Page 45	Double Woven Stitch Page 22	Waterfall Page 41	Banded Basket Stitch Page 18
Eyelets Page 28	Purled Ladder Stitch Page 15	Blanket Moss Stitch Page 31	Seed-Stitch Checks Page 24	Blanket Rib Page 31	Little Shell Pattern Page 42	Zigzag Stitch Page 20	Horizontal Two-One Ribs Page 12
King Charles Brocade Page 25	Vandyke Lace Panel 2 Page 36	Garter and Stockinette Cable Page 57	Rectangular Checks Page 19	Ridged Eyelet Border Page 26	Open Check Stitch Page 27	Eyelet Lattice Insertion Page 33	Mock Cable— Right Page 47
Harris-Tweed Rib Page 19	Piqué Check Stitch Page 13	Diagonal Rib 2 Page 20	Double Basket Weave Page 17	Single Lace Rib Page 38	Waffle Stitch Page 14	Garter Stitch Twisted Rib Page 32	Diamond Panel Page 44
Claw Pattern 1 Page 50	Simple Garter-Stitch Lace Page 30	Little Fountain Pattern Page 45	Bramble Stitch Page 32	Double Cable Page 51	Reverse Stockinette Chevron Page 26	Bluebell Rib Page 41	Vandyke Lace Panel 1 Page 35
Lattice Stitch Page 24	Staghorn Cable 2 Page 52	Eyelet Mock-Cable Rib Page 49	Eight-Stitch Cable Page 53	Fishtail Lace Panel Page 43	Allover Lattice Stitch Page 49	Check Pattern Page 14	Fish-Scale Lace Panel Page 37

Color A (Flame)

Color D (Silver Spruce Heather)

Color B (Mimosa)

Color E (Cobalt Heather)

Color C (Turquoise Heather)

Color F (Mystic Purple)

Small-Blocks Sampler Lap Robe

I used just three colors in this sampler for a subtle yet interesting blanket. Pick your favorite 36 stitch patterns and make it truly your own.

"Small-Blocks Sampler Lap Robe," designed and made by author

Skill Level

Intermediate ■■■□

Size

Approx 37" x 43" blocked; each block measures approx 6" x 7" blocked

Materials

Yarn: Cascade 220 by Cascade Yarns (100% wool; 100 g; 220 yds) *OR* an equivalent worsted-weight yarn (④)

- **A** 2 skeins in color 2452 (Turtle) *OR* approx 420 yds
- **B** 3 skeins in color 8013 (Walnut Heather) *OR* approx 575 yds
- **C** 2 skeins in color 4010 (Straw) *OR* approx 420 yds

Needles: Size 7 (4.5 mm) needles *OR* size needed to attain gauge; size G crochet hook for border

Gauge

20 sts and 28 rows = 4" in St st

Instructions

Make 36 small blocks. Choose pattern stitches of your own or see chart below for the stitches used in the sample shown on page 63.

> ### Doreen's Hint
>
> You can leave longer tails at both the cast-on and bind-off edges and use these for at least some of the seaming.

Finishing

Block each individual block to size. Lay out squares in sequence shown in chart. Seam together cast-on/bind-off edges of blocks using cast-on edge to bind-off edge assembly method (page 91) so that you will have 6 columns of blocks. Seam each column to next column using garter-stitch assembly method (page 91).

Outside Border

Using color of your choosing, work border of your choice around entire outside edge of afghan. The sample shown has a backward crochet border.
Weave in ends.

Small-Blocks Sampler Lap Robe—Block Placement

Rectangular Checks Page 19	Diagonal Rib 2 Page 20	Garter Stitch Twisted Rib Page 32	Single Lace Rib Page 38	Crocus Buds Page 29	Ridged Eyelet Border Page 26
Vandyke Lace Panel 1 Page 35	Waffle Stitch Page 14	Lattice Stitch Page 24	Check Pattern Page 14	Garter and Stockinette Cable Page 57	Harris-Tweed Rib Page 19
Stockinette Stitch Page 11	Garter-Stitch Ridges Page 11	Little Fountain Pattern Page 45	Bramble Stitch Page 32	Garter-Stitch Steps Page 18	Double Mock Rib Page 23
Blanket Rib Page 31	Zigzag Stitch Page 20	Eight-Stitch Cable Page 53	Horizontal Two-One Ribs Page 12	Sailors' Rib Page 21	Double Lace Rib Page 38
Bamboo Stitch Page 29	Double-Eyelet Rib Page 42	Little Shell Pattern Page 42	Seed-Stitch Checks Page 24	Mock-Cable Rib Page 48	Diagonal Seed Stitch Page 12
Feather Rib Page 46	Simple Garter-Stitch Lace Page 30	Corded Rib Page 33	Fleck Stitch Page 13	Fish-Scale Lace Panel Page 37	Staghorn Cable 2 Page 52

◻ Color A (Turtle)

◼ Color B (Walnut Heather)

◻ Color C (Straw)

Big-Blocks Sampler Afghan

Alternating a simple pattern block with a more complex one really showcases the more intricate patterns in some of the blocks. Limiting the number of squares lets you practice knitting more complex patterns without feeling overwhelmed by the quantity of blocks needed.

"Big-Blocks Sampler Afghan," designed and made by author

Skill Level

Easy ■■☐☐

Size

Approx 56" x 66" blocked; each block measures approx 11" x 13" blocked

Materials

Yarn: Vintage by Berroco (52% acrylic, 40% wool, 8% nylon; 100 g; 218 yds) *OR* an equivalent worsted-weight yarn (4)

A 4 skeins in color 5103 (Mocha) *OR* approx 775 yds

B 4 skeins in color 5105 (Oats) *OR* approx 775 yds

C 3 skeins in color 5104 (Mushroom) *OR* approx 560 yds

Needles: Size 8 (5 mm) needles *OR* size needed to attain gauge; size 8 (5 mm) 29" or longer circular needle and double-pointed needle for attached I-cord edging

Gauge

18 sts and 24 rows = 4" in St st

Instructions

Make 25 large blocks. See chart below for number of blocks to make in each pattern and color.

Finishing

Block each individual block to size. Lay out blocks in sequence shown in chart. Seam together cast-on/bind-off edges of blocks using cast-on edge to bind-off edge assembly method (page 91) so that you will have 5 columns of blocks. Seam each column to next column using garter-stitch assembly method (page 91).

Border

Using color B and long circular needle, with RS facing you, pick up stitches around perimeter of afghan, starting at bottom of right side edge of afghan, approx 2" in from corner. Work attached I-cord (page 91) around entire edge of afghan. Sew ends of I-cord together.

Weave in ends.

Big Blocks Sampler Afghan—Block Placement

Rectangular Checks Page 19	Stockinette Stitch Page 11	Bamboo Stitch Page 29	Fleck Stitch Page 13	Little Fountain Pattern Page 45
Fleck Stitch Page 13	Bramble Stitch Page 32	Fleck Stitch Page 13	Rectangular Checks Page 19	Stockinette Stitch Page 11
Little Fountain Pattern Page 45	Stockinette Stitch Page 11	Garter and Stockinette Cable Page 57	Stockinette Stitch Page 11	Bramble Stitch Page 32
Stockinette Stitch Page 11	Bamboo Stitch Page 29	Fleck Stitch Page 13	Little Fountain Pattern Page 45	Fleck Stitch Page 13
Bramble Stitch Page 32	Fleck Stitch Page 13	Rectangular Checks Page 19	Stockinette Stitch Page 11	Bamboo Stitch Page 29

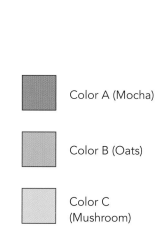

Color A (Mocha)

Color B (Oats)

Color C (Mushroom)

Single-Pattern
Afghans

Forked Cable Afghan

The Forked Cable is a rather nontraditional cable pattern. Whether you block this cable design or let it remain in its natural state, it will make a beautiful addition to any decor. Special thanks to Karen Kuckenbecker for knitting this design.

"Forked Cable Afghan," designed by author and made by Karen Kuckenbecker

Skill Level

Intermediate ■■■□

Size

Approx 38" x 48" unblocked, 40" x 50" blocked

Materials

Yarn: 12 skeins of Vintage Chunky from Berroco (52% acrylic, 40% wool, 8% nylon; 100 g; 130 yds) in color 6183 (Lilacs) *OR* approx 1450 yds of an equivalent chunky-weight yarn (5)

Needles: Size 10 (6 mm) circular needle (29" or longer) *OR* size required to attain gauge

Notions: Cable needle

Gauge

14 sts and 20 rows = 4" in St st

Stitch Pattern Used

Forked Cable, page 50

Instructions

CO 152 sts.

Knit 8 rows.

Inc row: K7, *K3, M1, K4; rep from * to last 5 sts, K5—172 sts.

Keeping first and last 5 sts in garter stitch, work rows 1–10 of Forked Cable patt over rem 162 sts.

Doreen's Note

This is one of those exception-to-the-rule stitches wherein the odd-numbered rows are actually the *wrong* side of the knitted fabric. This tends to confuse some knitters at first, but once you get through a repeat, you should be fine.

Rep rows 1–10 until afghan measures approx 45" from beg or approx 2" less than desired finished length, end with row 10.

Work rows 1–5 once more.

Dec row: K5, K1, *K3, K2tog, K3; rep from * to last 6 sts, K1, K5—152 sts.

Knit 6 rows.

BO kw on WS.

Finishing

Weave in all loose ends. Block if desired.

Banded Basket Stitch Afghan

I absolutely love reversible pattern stitches for afghans, and this is one of my favorites. Whether done in a solid color or a beautiful variegated yarn as shown here, this blanket is surely one that will be cuddled under on a cold evening.

"Banded Basket Stitch Afghan," designed and made by author

Skill Level

Beginner ■□□□

Size

Approx 38" x 46" blocked

Materials

Yarn: 7 skeins of Rios from Malabrigo Yarn (100% pure merino superwash wool; 100 g; 210 yds) in color 866 (Arco Iris) *OR* approx 1470 yds of an equivalent worsted-weight yarn 🔢

Needles: Size 8 (5 mm) 29" or longer needle *OR* size needed to attain gauge

Gauge

17 sts and 26 rows = 4" in St st

Stitch Pattern Used

Banded Basket Stitch, page 18

Bottom Border

CO 182 sts. Work seed st border as follows:

Row 1: *K1, P1; rep from * across row.

Row 2: *P1, K1; rep from * across row.

Rep rows 1 and 2 another 4 times for a total of 10 border rows.

Body of Afghan

Keeping first and last 7 sts in seed st as established, work rows 1–10 of Banded Basket Stitch patt over rem 168 sts. Rep rows 1–10 until afghan measures approx 44" from beg, end with row 10.

Top Border

Row 1: *K1, P1; rep from * across row.

Row 2: *P1, K1; rep from * across row.

Rep rows 1 and 2 another 4 times for a total of 10 border rows.

BO in patt on RS.

Finishing

Weave in any loose ends. Block if desired.

Broken-Rib Diagonal Afghan

This afghan looks great no matter which side you choose as the "right" side. The pattern stitch is simple enough for the beginning knitter, yet has enough going on to keep the interest of even the more advanced knitter. I've played around with the stitch pattern slightly to add a little "zig" to the design. Plus, the math has been done here for you so you can choose from baby size, lap-robe size, or full-sized afghan.

"Broken-Rib Diagonal Afghan," designed and made by author

Skill Level

Beginner ■□□□

Size

Baby: Approx 29" x 33" blocked
Lap robe: Approx 38" x 44" blocked
Afghan: Approx 46" x 55" blocked

Materials

Yarn: 5 (8, 10) skeins of Pediboo Worsted by Frog Tree Yarns (80% superwash merino wool, 20% bamboo; 100 g; 182 yds) in color 1337 *OR* approx 825 (1375, 1750) yds of an equivalent worsted-weight yarn ④

Needles: Size 7 (4.5 mm) 29" or longer needle *OR* size needed to attain gauge

Gauge

19 sts and 28 rows = 4" in St st

Stitch Pattern Used

Broken-Rib Diagonal, page 21

Instructions

Instructions are written for the baby-blanket size with the larger sizes shown in parentheses.

CO 140 (180, 220) sts.

Knit 6 (8, 10) rows for bottom border.

Keeping first and last 4 (6, 8) sts in garter st as established, work Broken-Rib Diagonal patt over rem 132 (168, 204) sts as follows:

Work 6 (8, 10) reps of rows 1–12 of Broken-Rib Diagonal patt for a total of 72 (92, 120) rows.

Then work 6 (8, 10) reps of the patt rows working rows 1–4, 9–12, then 5–8 for a total of 72 (92, 120) more rows.

Work 6 (8, 10) reps of rows 1–12 for a total of 72 (92, 120) more rows.

Knit 6 (8, 10) rows for top border.

BO kw on RS.

Finishing

Weave in ends. Block if desired.

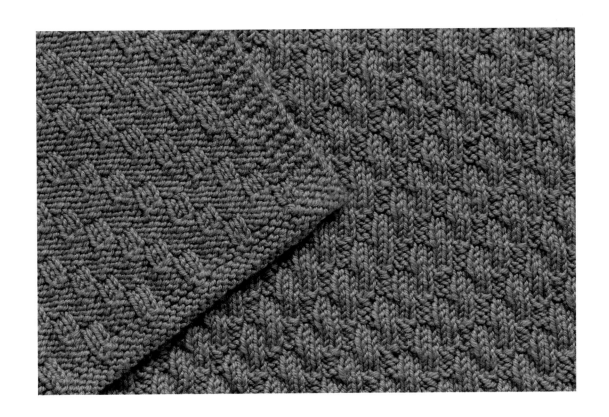

Vertically Patterned
Afghans

Choosing Stitch Patterns for Vertical Designs

You can combine any number of stitch patterns and work them vertically to make an afghan that is totally your own design. There are two ways to knit this type of afghan. You can knit strips of different stitch patterns, making sure they are all the same number of rows, and then sew them together, or you can knit the afghan all in one piece. In the second method you'll have to keep track of which row of the repeat you are on for each stitch pattern chosen. Therefore, it may be easier for you to select patterns that either have the same number of rows in a pattern repeat or make yourself a little chart to keep track of which row you are on for each respective stitch pattern. It definitely takes a little more concentration to construct the afghan all in one piece, but you won't have anything to seam together when you are done knitting.

This is also where stitch markers will come in handy. Place them to separate each stitch pattern used. This helps immensely in making sure you are on track with each pattern. It's much easier to back up a few stitches than to reach the end of the row and find out you made a mistake near the beginning of the row.

If you combine different stitch types, don't forget to add/subtract stitches when going from the border to the body of the piece as was done in the individual sample blocks. This will ensure that your borders lie flat when finished. Then, of course, you need to do the opposite before starting the top border so that you are back to the original number of cast-on stitches.

Vandyke Lace Afghan

Who would have thought that combining just two different lace patterns could make such a stunning afghan? By varying the placement and number of repeats of the stitch patterns, a beautiful and intricate-looking (yet easy to achieve) afghan results.

"Vandyke Lace Afghan," designed and made by author

Skill Level

Intermediate ■■■□

Size

Approx 40" x 48" blocked

Materials

Yarn: 10 skeins of Kenzie by Hikoo (50% New Zealand merino, 25% nylon, 10% angora, 10% alpaca, 5% silk noils; 50 g; 160 yds) in color 1006 (Kumara) *OR* approx 1600 yds of an equivalent DK-weight yarn ⟨3⟩

Needles: Size 6 (4 mm) 29" or longer needle *OR* size needed to attain gauge

Notions: Stitch markers

Gauge

22 sts and 30 rows = 4" in St st

Stitch Patterns Used

Vandyke Lace Panel 1, page 35
Vandyke Lace Panel 2, page 36

Bottom Border

CO 199 sts.

Rows 1–6: K1, *P1, K1; rep from * across row.

Set-up row 1 (RS): K1, (P1, K1) twice, pm, K6, pm, K9, pm, K7, pm, K17, pm, K3, pm, K9, pm, K3, pm, K17, pm, K7, pm, K9, pm, K3, pm; K9, pm, K3, pm; K9, pm, K7, pm, K17, pm, K3, pm, K9, pm, K3, pm, K17, pm, K7, pm, K9, pm, K6, pm, K1, (P1, K1) twice.

Set-up row 2: K1, (P1, K1) twice, purl to last 5 sts, slipping markers as you come to them, K1, (P1, K1) twice.

Keeping Track of Your Knitting

Although using so many markers may seem a bit much, you'll be thankful when you start the pattern stitches. You can always remove some markers when you become more familiar with the pattern. However, the markers serve as a nice checkpoint to make sure you're on track with each pattern. Better to have to rip back only a few stitches than an entire row.

Body of Afghan

Row 1 (RS): K1, (P1, K1) twice, K6, work row 1 of Vandyke Lace Panel 2 over next 9 sts, K7, work row 1 of Vandyke Lace Panel 1 over next 17 sts, K3, work row 1 of Vandyke Lace Panel 2 over next 9 sts, K3, work row 1 of Vandyke Lace Panel 1 over next 17 sts, K7, (work row 1 of Vandyke Lace Panel 2 over next 9 sts, K3) twice, work row 1 of Vandyke Lace Panel 2 over next 9 sts, K7, work row 1 of Vandyke Lace Panel 1 over next 17 sts, K3, work row 1 of Vandyke Lace Panel 2 over next 9 sts, K3, work row 1 of Vandyke Lace Panel 1 over next 17 sts, K7, work row 1 of Vandyke Lace Panel 2 over next 9 sts, K6, K1, (P1, K1) twice.

Vandyke Lace Panel 1

Border   Vandyke Lace Panel 2   Border

Row 2: K1, (P1, K1) twice, P6, work row 2 of Vandyke Lace Panel 2, P7, work row 2 of Vandyke Lace Panel 1, P3, work row 2 of Vandyke Lace Panel 2, P3, work row 2 of Vandyke Lace Panel 1, P7, (work row 2 of Vandyke Lace Panel 2, P3) twice, work row 2 of Vandyke Lace Panel 2, P7, work row 2 of Vandyke Lace Panel 1, P3, work row 2 of Vandyke Lace Panel 2, P3, work row 2 of Vandyke Lace Panel 1, P7, work row 2 of Vandyke Lace Panel 2, P6, K1 (P1, K1) twice.

Keeping first and last 5 sts in seed stitch, cont working lace panels as established, keeping sts between the sets of panels in St st as established. Cont repeating the patts until you have completed a total of 312 patt rows.

Next row: K1, (P1, K1) twice, knit to last 5 sts, K1, (P1, K1) twice.

Next row: K1, (P1, K1) twice, purl to last 5 sts, K1, (P1, K1) twice.

Top Border

Work 6 rows in seed stitch as you did for the bottom border.

BO kw on RS.

Finishing

Weave in ends. Block to size.

Triple Cable Afghan

By knitting this cabled afghan in strips, it's much easier to keep track of where you are in each cable pattern, thus making the project a much less daunting undertaking. Keeping narrow garter-stitch borders on each strip makes seaming a breeze and virtually invisible.

"Triple Cable Afghan," designed and made by author

Skill Level

Intermediate ■■■□

Size

Approx 46" x 54" blocked

Materials

Yarn: 3 skeins of Rustic Aran Tweed from James C. Brett (77% acrylic, 20% wool, 3% viscose; 400 g; 760 yds) in color DAT5 *OR* approx 1800 yds of an equivalent worsted-weight yarn (4)

Needles: Size 9 (5.5 mm) 29" or longer needle *OR* size needed to attain gauge

Notions: Cable needle

Gauge

16 sts and 20 rows = 4" in St st

Stitch Patterns Used

Double Cable, page 51
Eight-Stitch Cable, page 53
Knotted Cable, page 54

Center Panel

Make 1.

CO 49 sts.

Bottom Border

Rows 1, 3, and 5 (RS): Knit.

Rows 2, 4, and 6: K3, P1, K41, P1, K3.

Set-up row 1 (RS): K4, P3, (K1, M1, K2) 3 times, P4, (K1, M1, K2) 3 times, P4, (K1, M1, K2) 3 times, P3, K4—58 sts.

Set-up row 2: K3, P1, K3, P12, K4, P12, K4, P12, K3, P1, K3.

Body of Panel

Row 1 (RS): K4, P3, work row 1 of Upward Double Cable patt over next 12 sts, P4, work row 1 of Downward Double Cable patt over next 12 sts, P4, work row 1 of Upward Double Cable patt over next 12 sts, P3, K4.

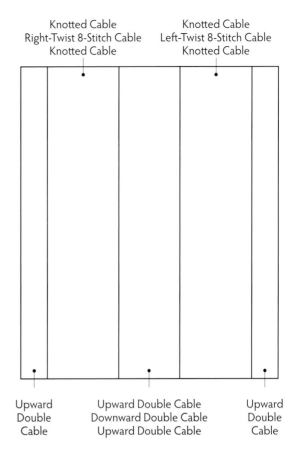

Knotted Cable — Right-Twist 8-Stitch Cable — Knotted Cable

Knotted Cable — Left-Twist 8-Stitch Cable — Knotted Cable

Upward Double Cable

Upward Double Cable — Downward Double Cable — Upward Double Cable

Upward Double Cable

Row 2: K3, P1, K3, work row 2 of Upward Double Cable patt, K4, work row 2 of Downward Double Cable patt, K4, work row 2 of Upward Double Cable patt, K3, P1, K3.

Rows 3–8: Keeping first and last 4 sts in garter stitch, cont working lace panels as established, keeping sts between cables in rev St st as established.

Rep rows 1–8 a total of 36 times, ending the last rep after working row 6.

Next row (RS): K4, *P3, (K1, K2tog, K1) 3 times; P4, (K1, K2tog, K1) 3 times; P4, (K1, K2tog, K1) 3 times; P3, K4—49 sts.

Next row: K3, P1, K3, P9, K4, P9, K4, P9, K3, P1, K3.

Top Border

Rows 1, 3, and 5 (RS): Knit.

Rows 2, 4, and 6: K3, P1, K41, P1, K3.

BO kw on RS.

Side Panel

Make 2.

CO 57 sts.

Bottom Border

Rows 1, 3, and 5 (RS): Knit.

Rows 2, 4, and 6: K3, P1, K10, P1, K2, P1, K21, P1, K2, P1, K10, P1, K3.

Set-up row 1 (RS): K4, P3, K1, M1, P2, M1, K1, P3, K4, P3, K2, (M1, K2) twice, P3, K2, (M1, K2) twice, P3, K4, P3, M1, K1, P2, M1, K1; P3, K4—65 sts.

Set-up row 2: K3, P1, K3, P2, K2, P2, K3, P1, K2, P1, K3, P8, K3, P8, K3, P1, K2, P1, K3, P2, K2, P2, K3, P1, K3.

> ### Doreen's Hint
>
> In order to make the side cable panels symmetrical, work right-twist Eight-Stitch Cables on one side panel and left-twist Eight-Stitch Cables on the other.

Body of Panel

Row 1 (RS): K4, P3, work row 1 of Knotted Cable patt over next 6 sts, P3, K4, P3, work row 1 of Eight-Stitch Cable over next 8 sts, P3, work row 1 of Eight-Stitch Cable over next 8 sts, P3, K4, P3, work row 1 of Knotted Cable over next 6 sts, P3, K4.

Row 2: K3, P1, K3, work row 2 of Knotted Cable, K3, P1, K2, P1, K3, work row 2 of Eight-Stitch Cable, P3, work row 2 of Eight-Stitch Cable, K3, P1, K2, P1, K3, work row 2 of Knotted Cable, K3, P1, K3.

Rows 3–10: Keeping first and last 3 sts in garter stitch, cont working cable panels as established, keeping sts between cables in patts as established.

Rep rows 1–10 a total of 28 times and then work rows 1–6 once more.

Next row: K4, P3, K2tog, P2, K2tog, P3, K4, P3, (K1, K2tog, K2, K2tog, K1, P3) twice, K4, P3, K2tog, P2, K2tog, P3, K4—57 sts.

Top Border

Knit 5 rows.

BO kw on RS.

End Panel

Make 2.

CO 23 sts.

Bottom Border

Rows 1, 3, and 5 (RS): Knit.

Rows 2, 4, and 6: K3, P1, K15, P1, K3.

Set-up row 1 (RS): K4, P3, (K1, M1, K2) three times, P3, K4—26 sts.

Set-up row 2: K3, P1, K3, P12, K3, P1, K3.

Body of Panel

Row 1 (RS): K4, P3, work row 1 of Upward Double Cable over next 12 sts, P3, K4.

Row 2: K3, P1, K3, work row 2 of Upward Double Cable, K3, P1, K3.

Rows 3–8: Keeping first and last 3 sts in garter stitch, cont working cable panel as established, keeping sts each side of cable in patt as established.

Rep rows 1–8 a total of 36 times, ending last rep after working row 6.

Next row: K4, P3, (K1, K2tog, K1) three times, P3, K4—23 sts.

Next row: K3, P1, K3, P9, K3, P1, K3.

Top Border

Knit 5 rows.

BO kw on RS.

Finishing

Block panels if desired. Seam panels together using the garter-stitch assembly method (page 91). See illustration (page 79) for panel layout. Weave in any ends.

> ### Doreen's Hint
>
> It's much easier to block the panels individually before seaming them together than it is to block the entire blanket.

Paprika Lou Afghan

Combining just three different stitch patterns can create such a beautiful result. While it will require a little more work to keep track of which row you're on for each pattern, the outcome is well worth the effort. While I was knitting this afghan, thoughts of my father kept coming to mind. The Tile Stitch reminds me of bricks; he was a bricklayer by trade. He was also an avid fisherman, and the four-stitch cable . . . well, he did have four children! I just had to name the afghan in his memory.

"Paprika Lou Afghan," designed and made by author

Skill Level

Intermediate ■■■□

Size

Approx 42" x 48" blocked

Materials

Yarn: 8 skeins of Exuberance - DK from Claudia Hand Painted Yarns (100% superwash merino wool; 100 g; 225 yds) in color Paprika *OR* approx 1800 yds of an equivalent DK-weight yarn ③

Needles: Size 6 (4 mm) 29" or longer needle *OR* size needed to attain gauge

Notions: Stitch markers

Gauge

22 sts and 30 rows = 4" in St st

Stitch Patterns Used

Four-Stitch Cable 2, page 58
Fish-Scale Lace Panel, page 37
Tile Stitch, page 17

Instructions

CO 238 sts.

Row 1 (RS): K10, pm, P4, work row 1 of Four-Stitch Cable 2 patt over next 4 sts, P3, work row 1 of Four-Stitch Cable 2 patt over next 4 sts, P4, pm, K2, (work row 1 of Fish-Scale Lace Panel over next 17 sts) twice, K2, pm, P4, work row 1 of Four-Stitch Cable 2 patt over next 4 sts, P3, work row 1 of Four-Stitch Cable 2 patt over next 4 sts, P3, work row 1 of Four-Stitch Cable 2 patt over next 4 sts, P4, pm, work next 52 sts in Tile Stitch, pm, P4, work row 1 of Four-Stitch Cable 2 patt over next 4 sts, P3, work row 1 of Four-Stitch Cable 2 patt over next 4 sts, P3, work row 1 of Four-Stitch Cable 2 patt over next 4 sts, P4, pm, K2, (work row 1 of Fish-Scale Lace Panel over next 17 sts) twice, K2, pm, P4, work row 1 of Four-Stitch Cable 2 patt over next 4 sts, P3, work row 1 of Four-Stitch Cable 2 patt over next 4 sts, P4, pm, K10.

Row 2: K3, P2, K3, P2, sm, K4, work row 2 of Four-Stitch Cable 2 patt over next 4 sts, K3, work row 2 of Four-Stitch Cable 2 patt over next 4 sts, K4, sm, P2, (work row 2 of Fish-Scale Lace Panel over next 17 sts) twice, P2, sm, K4, work row 2 of Four-Stitch Cable 2 patt over next 4 sts, K3, work row 2 of Four-Stitch Cable 2 patt over next 4 sts, K3, work row 2 of Four-Stitch Cable 2 patt over next 4 sts, K4, sm, work next 52 sts in Tile Stitch, sm, K4, work row 2 of Four-Stitch Cable 2 patt over next 4 sts, K3, work row 2 of Four-Stitch Cable 2 patt over next 4 sts, P3, work row 2 of Four-Stitch Cable 2 patt over next 4 sts, K4, sm, P2, (work row 2 of Fish-Scale Lace Panel over next 17 sts) twice, P2, sm, K4, work row 2 of Four-Stitch Cable 2 patt over next 4 sts, K3, work row 2 of Four-Stitch Cable 2 patt over next 4 sts, K4, sm, K3, P2, K3, P2.

Cont working patts as established, until afghan measures approx 48" from beg, end last set of row reps on row 3 of the Four-Stitch Cable 2 patt and row 7 of both the Tile Stitch and Fish-Scale Lace Panel patts. BO in pattern on WS.

Doreen's Hint

For a longer afghan, add on additional rows in multiples of 8 in order to complete full pattern repeats.

Finishing

Weave in loose ends. Block if desired.

Horizontally Patterned
Afghans

Choosing Stitch Patterns for Horizontal Rows

You can easily combine a multitude of stitch patterns into one afghan. You just have to make sure that the number of stitches in a pattern repeat all fit into the number of stitches that you've cast on. It may be necessary to knit a horizontal border in between each pattern section where you can make increases or decreases to make a particular pattern fit. If one pattern has a couple more or fewer stitches than another, the difference can easily be blocked out and will not even be noticeable. Just remember that some stitches will draw in the knitted fabric (such as cables), while others will relax the knitted fabric more (such as lace), and you'll have to plan the number of stitches to increase/decrease accordingly.

Shady Banks Afghan

Combining some basic stitch patterns makes an afghan that's anything but basic. Rich with texture and the color variations of kettle-dyed yarn, this project is sure to become your favorite afghan to wrap up in on chilly evenings.

"Shady Banks Afghan," designed and made by author

Skill Level

Beginner ■□□□

Size

Approx 42" x 54" blocked

Materials

Yarn: 8 skeins of Rios from Malabrigo Yarn (100% pure merino superwash wool; 100 g; 210 yds) in color 131 (Sand Bank) OR approx 1680 yds of an equivalent worsted-weight yarn (4)

Needles: Size 8 (5 mm) 29" or longer needle OR size needed to attain gauge

Gauge

17 sts and 26 rows = 4" in St st

Stitch Patterns Used

Garter-Stitch Steps, page 18
Piqué Check Stitch, page 13
Waffle Stitch, page 14
Zigzag Stitch, page 20

Instructions

CO 178 sts.

Purl 10 rows.

Keeping first and last 5 sts in purl garter st as established, work body of afghan over rem 168 sts as follows:

Section 1

Work 3 reps of rows 1–16 (48 rows) of Garter-Stitch Steps patt ending with a WS row. Purl 6 rows.

Section 2

Work rows 1–24 of Piqué Check Stitch patt and then work rows 1–18 once more for a total of 42 rows. Purl 6 rows, inc 1 st at center of last row—169 patt sts.

Section 3

Work 8 reps of rows 1–4 (32 rows) of Waffle Stitch patt and then work rows 1–3 once more for a total of 35 rows and thus ending with a RS row. Purl 7 rows, dec 1 st at center of first row—168 patt sts.

Section 4

Work 5 reps of rows 1–12 of Zigzag Stitch patt for a total of 60 rows.

Purl 6 rows, inc 1 st at center of last row—169 patt sts.

Section 5

Rep section 3.

Section 6

Rep section 2, omitting increase on last row—168 patt sts.

Section 7

Rep section 1.

Purl 3 rows thus ending with a RS row.

BO pw on WS.

Reality Check

Purling 3 rows after completing section 7 will give you a total of 9 purl rows for the bottom border.

Finishing

Weave in all ends. Block.

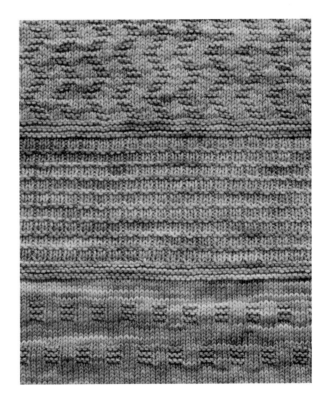

Lacy Layers Afghan

Whether you knit this design using two colors as I did, or use just one color throughout, it's a design that's great for trying various lace-stitch patterns. Garter rows between each lace section not only serve to separate the pattern stitches, but they make the perfect spot to do any increasing or decreasing necessary to accommodate the next pattern stitch being used.

"Lacy Layers Afghan," designed and made by author

Skill Level

Easy ■■□□

Size

Approx 46" x 63" blocked

Materials

Yarn: Tempo from Jojoland (80% acrylic, 20% wool; 100 g; 195 yds) *OR* an equivalent worsted-weight yarn (**4**)

- A 5 skeins in color 544 (blue) *OR* approx 975 yds
- B 4 skeins in color 576 (green) *OR* approx 750 yds

Needles: Size 7 (4.5 mm) 29" or longer needle *OR* size needed to attain gauge

Gauge

16 sts and 28 rows = 4" in garter st

> **Stitch Patterns Used**
>
> Single-Eyelet Rib, page 39
> Lacy Checks, page 46
> Little Shell Pattern, page 42
> Bluebell Rib, page 41

Border

Using A, CO 170 sts. Knit 6 rows.

Body of Afghan

The body of the afghan is worked in 7 sections.

Section 1

Keeping first and last 4 sts in garter stitch, work rows 1–8 of Single-Eyelet Rib patt over rem 162 sts. Rep rows 1–8 another 5 times for a total of 48 patt rows. Knit 2 rows. Cut A.

Section 2

Attach B. Knit 2 rows, dec 1 st at center of second row—169 sts.

Keeping first and last 4 sts in garter stitch, cont over rem 161 sts as follows:

Set-up row 1: Knit.

Set-up row 2: Purl.

Work rows 1–12 of Lacy Checks patt. Rep rows 1–12 twice; then work rows 1–10 once more for a total of 46 patt rows (not including the set-up rows). Knit 2 rows. Cut B.

Section 3

Attach A. Knit 2 rows, inc 2 sts evenly over second row—171 sts.

Keeping first and last 4 sts in garter stitch, work rows 1–4 of Little Shell patt over rem 163 sts. Rep rows 1–4 another 11 times for a total of 48 patt rows. Knit 2 rows. Cut A.

Section 4

Attach B. Knit 2 rows, dec 1 st at center of second row—170 sts.

Keeping first and last 4 sts in garter stitch, work rows 1–6 of Bluebell Rib patt over rem 162 sts.

Rep rows 1–6 another 7 times; then work rows 1 and 2 once more for a total of 50 patt rows. Knit 2 rows. Cut B.

Section 5

Attach A. Knit 2 rows, inc 1 st at center of second row—171 sts.

Keeping first and last 4 sts in garter stitch, work rows 1–4 of Little Shell patt over rem 163 sts. Rep rows 1–4 another 11 times for a total of 48 patt rows. Knit 2 rows. Cut A.

Section 6

Attach B. Knit 2 rows, dec 2 sts evenly over second row—169 sts.

Keeping first and last 4 sts in garter stitch, cont over rem 161 sts as follows:

Set-up row 1 (RS): Knit.

Set-up row 2: Purl.

Work rows 1–12 of Lacy Checks patt. Rep rows 1–12 twice; then work rows 1–10 once more for a total of 46 patt rows (not including the set-up rows). Knit 2 rows. Cut B.

Section 7

Attach A. Knit 2 rows, inc 1 st at center of second row—170 sts.

Keeping first and last 4 sts in garter stitch, work rows 1–8 of Single-Eyelet Rib patt over rem 162 sts. Rep rows 1–8 another 5 times for 48 total patt rows.

Top Border

Knit 6 rows. BO loosely knitwise on RS.

Finishing

Weave in loose ends. Block.

Knitting Basics

Refer to the following guidelines for basic techniques used for projects in this book.

Basic Pattern Stitches

Most of the designs in this book use these basic pattern stitches.

Garter stitch. Knit every row.

Stockinette stitch. Knit the right-side rows, purl the wrong-side rows.

Cast Ons

While there is no particular cast on that is absolutely necessary to accomplish the blocks in this book, the following is my favorite.

Long-Tail Cast On— Using One Ball of Yarn

This is one of the most common methods of casting on. It is very easy to do and provides some elasticity at the edge. As the name implies, you have a long tail of yarn from which to start this method and you'll be using both the tail and the working yarn to cast on.

The trickiest part of this cast on is determining how much yarn to leave at the tail end. A basic rule of thumb is to figure approximately 1" per stitch. This amount works well for worsted-weight yarns on a size 7 or 8 needle. If you're using finer yarns and smaller needles, then it will take a little less; likewise if you're using larger needles and heavier yarn, it will take more. Once you have done the long-tail cast on a few times, you'll get the hang of how much yarn to leave at the tail end.

1. Leaving a long tail, make a slipknot and place it on the needle. With the needle in the right hand, insert the left thumb and index finger between the strands and spread them apart with

the tail of the yarn over your index finger and the working yarn over your thumb.

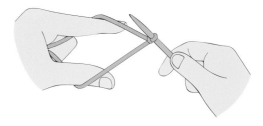

2. Turn the thumb and index finger up to wrap the tail around the thumb and the working strand around the finger. Hold both ends in the fingers of the left hand.

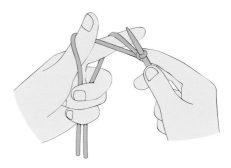

3. Insert the needle into the front of thumb loop going in from the bottom.

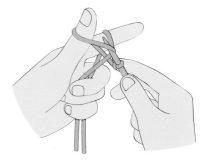

4. Go over the top of the loop on the index finger with the needle.

5. Pull the strand back down through the thumb loop.

6. Remove the thumb from the loop, insert the thumb between the strands, and tug the tail to gently tighten the stitch. Repeat from step 2 for the required number of stitches.

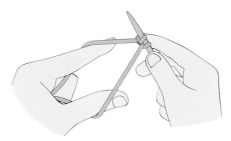

Long-Tail Cast On— Using Two Balls of Yarn

If you're casting on a large number of stitches, such as for the entire width of an afghan, it's sometimes difficult to predetermine just how much yarn you are going to need on the tail. It's very discouraging to cast on almost enough stitches only to realize that you don't have quite enough yarn left on the tail end to finish. The following method will prevent this from happening.

1. Using a strand of yarn each from two different skeins of yarn, make a slipknot and slip it onto your needle. With this method, the slipknot does not count as a stitch. The slipknot will be dropped off the needle on the first row.

2. With the needle in the right hand, insert the left thumb and index finger between the strands and spread them apart. It doesn't make any difference which strand goes in the front or the back as they are both coming from full skeins of yarn and there's no way you will run out of either.

Continue as for the regular long-tail cast on. When you've cast on the required number of stitches, simply cut one of the strands . . . again it doesn't really make a difference which one. Just make sure you leave a 4" to 6" tail for weaving in.

Increases

While there are numerous methods for increasing stitches, following are the recommended methods for the designs in this book.

Knit in Front and Back of Stitch (K1f&b)

This is one of the most basic and easiest ways to increase. Simply knit into the stitch you want to increase in as you normally would, only don't take the stitch off either needle.

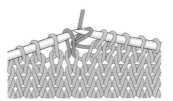

Knit into stitch but do not
drop it off left needle.

Bring the right needle around to the back of your work and knit that same stitch again, this time going into the back loop of the stitch and dropping the "old" stitch off the left needle.

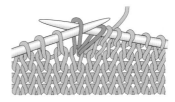

Knit into back of same stitch.

Be aware that this type of increase will result in one normal-looking stitch and one stitch that will have a horizontal bar going across it. You didn't do anything wrong. That's just how this increase looks. Usually this little bar doesn't cause any problems, but on occasion it does take away from the look of the garment, and you may want to opt for a different increase method.

Make One Stitch (M1)

The make-one increase lets you avoid the horizontal bar of the K1f&b increase. There are two ways in which to M1. One will slant to the left, while the other will slant to the right. If the directions don't specify "M1L" or "M1R," it really won't make any difference which one you do. Try both and at those times, simply use the one that is easiest for you to accomplish.

Make One Stitch Left (M1L)

When correctly done, the make-one increase is virtually invisible. Work up to the point where the increase is supposed to go. Pick up the horizontal strand between the stitch just worked and the next stitch by inserting the left needle from front to back and placing the strand on the left needle. Now, knit this stitch through the back loop.

You'll notice that you're actually twisting this stitch to the left as you knit it. If you don't twist the stitch you'll make a hole where the bar was picked up. By knitting into the back of the stitch, you eliminate the hole.

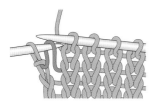 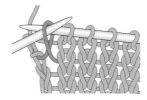

Pick up horizontal strand from front to back.　　Knit into back of stitch.

Make One Stitch Right (M1R)

This increase is done almost exactly like the M1L except that you pick up the horizontal strand by inserting the left needle from back to front, placing the strand on the left needle. You then knit the stitch through the front loop (as normal).

This increase will twist the stitch to the right as you knit it.

 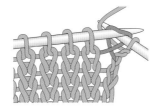

Pick up horizontal strand from back to front.　　Knit into front of stitch.

Decreases

While there are many ways to decrease, the following methods were used in this book.

Knit Two Stitches Together (K2tog)

This is a right-slanting decrease; when you're done, the stitches will slant toward the right. Instead of knitting the next stitch on the left needle as usual, insert the right needle from left to right through the second stitch and then through the first stitch on the left-hand needle and knit them as one stitch.

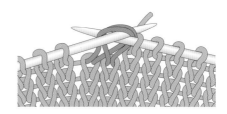

Slip, Slip, Knit (ssk)

This is a left-slanting decrease; when you're done, the stitches slant to the left. It's a mirror image of the K2tog decrease. Work up to where the decrease is to be done. Slip the next two stitches individually, as if to knit, onto the right-hand needle.

Insert the left-hand needle into the front part of the stitches, going from left to right, and knit these two stitches together, making one stitch out of two.

Move two slipped stitches to left needle.

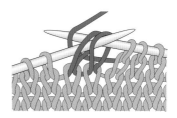

Knit two stitches together.

Use the following techniques to assemble the blocks. Feel free to use your favorite techniques if you prefer.

Joining Cast-On Edges to Bind-Off Edges

Lay blocks to be joined face up on a table with the bound-off edge of one block next to the cast-on edge of the block that's going to be placed above it. Using the yarn from either block (or a new piece) and a tapestry needle, bring the needle up through the center of a stitch at the edge of the lower block. On the other block, pick up two strands of yarn, inserting the needle in the space between stitches. Going back to the lower block, pick up two strands of yarn inserting the needle into the center of the stitch. For each stitch, insert the needle in the space where the last stitch on that block came out.

Adjust the tension so the sewn stitches are the same size as the knitted stitches. This seam should look like an extra row of knitting on top of the cast-on/bound-off edges.

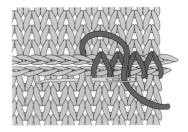

Garter-Stitch Assembly

When stitching two sections together that are both garter stitch, I use the following approach.

With right side facing you, lay the two pieces with the edges that need to be joined next to each other. Thread a piece of matching yarn or use the tail from your cast on (if you happened to leave a long enough one). Insert the needle through the very bottom loop of your cast on from one of the pieces; immediately insert the needle through the very bottom loop of your cast on from the other side and pull it through. This secures the pieces, and you are set to continue.

Now, when you look at your knitting you will notice that there is an "upper" loop to each garter stitch as well as a "lower" loop. Alternating from one side to the other, proceed as follows: Insert the needle from bottom to top in the lower loop on one side and the upper loop on the other side, pull yarn through, and even the tension out to match that of your knitting.

It doesn't make any difference which side you're taking the lower or upper loop from, just make sure that you're alternating loops. By doing this, you won't be able to even see where your seam is once you finish. At first it may seem that you are going over too far on one side, but don't let this alarm you. The blocks will all lie flat and look fantastic in the end. This technique will leave just a small ridge on the wrong side.

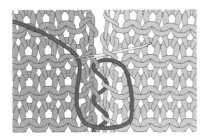

Blanket Borders

Adding a border to the finished blanket gives the project that extra finishing touch. This is especially nice on sampler afghans and afghans made with vertical panels, as it smooths out the edges and ties all of the pieces together into a unified whole. Here are two techniques that I like to use to finish off my blankets.

Attached I-Cord

Attached I-cord makes a wonderful border for afghans. While it may seem a little awkward to do at first, once you get the hang of it, you'll be able to do it quite proficiently. The width of the I-cord is determined by the extra number of stitches that you cast on and will vary depending on the weight of yarn you are using. Generally speaking, four stitches is a good number to start with.

With the right side facing you, using the long circular needle and starting at the bottom of the right-side edge of the afghan (approximately 2" in from the corner), begin picking up stitches around the entire edge of the afghan.

When you have a fair amount of stitches on the needle, take a second strand of yarn and use it to cast on four stitches to the tip of the needle that is at the end you *began* picking up stitches. Using a double-pointed needle as the second needle, begin working the attached I-cord as follows:

* Knit 3 sts, K2tog.

Do not turn the work. Slide the four stitches from the right-hand needle back over to the left-hand needle.

Repeat from *, making sure the yarn is pulled snugly behind when brought from the last stitch worked in the previous row to the first stitch worked in the current row.

Note that the first stitch you knit in the previous row is also the first stitch you knit in every row. The yarn is pulled across the back each time to start the new row. After three or four rows, you'll notice that you're actually forming a cord. You will also note that in each row you're knitting three of the four stitches you cast on and then knitting stitch number four together with one stitch from all those that you picked up around the afghan edge.

If your cord is loose, it's most likely because the yarn is not being pulled tightly enough across the back when you begin each row.

When you use up the stitches that are on the circular needle, simple pick up more, remembering to go back to using the strand of yarn that was started for that purpose. Continue in this method until the I-cord has been applied around the entire perimeter of the afghan. Bind off the remaining four stitches. Sew the cast-on and bound-off edges of the I-cord together. Weave in any loose ends.

Doreen's Hint

In order to make nice square corners on the afghan, work two rows of I-cord *not* attaching it to the afghan in the very tip of each corner. To do this, just knit the 4 stitches, place them back onto the left-hand needle, and knit them again. Then, continue in the usual manner of attaching once again.

Backward Crochet Border

Backward crochet (sometimes called reverse crochet, crab stitch, or knurl stitch) is a particularly nice way to edge an afghan. It gives a finished look.

Select a hook size that is appropriate for the yarn you're using. With the right side facing you, work a row of single crochet evenly around the outside edge of the afghan. You may have to skip a stitch here and there to make sure that the work lies flat. When you get to the corners, work two or three single crochet stitches in the very corner stitch.

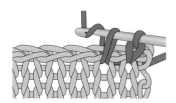

Insert hook into stitch, yarn over hook, pull loop through to front, yarn over hook.

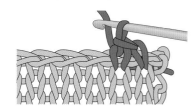

Pull loop through both loops on hook.

When you reach the starting point of the row of single crochet, join with a slip stitch into the first single crochet you made on the edging. DO NOT TURN YOUR WORK. Chain one.

Now, working in the direction opposite from what you normally do, work a second row of single crochet over the row you just made. Notice that you have formed a lovely row of firm loops over the top of the crocheting. If your loops are uneven, try again. This technique takes a little practice, but it's well worth the effort.

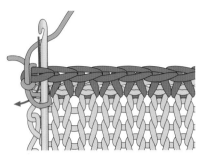

Join yarn with slip stitch. Insert hook into first stitch to the right.

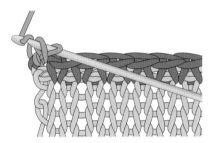

Yarn over hook, pull through both loops on hook.

Cable Techniques

Cable 4 back (C4B): Slip next 2 stitches onto the cable needle and hold at the back of the work. Knit the next 2 stitches from the left-hand needle; then knit 2 stitches from the cable needle.

Cable 4 front (C4F): Slip the next 2 stitches onto the cable needle and hold at the front of your work. Knit the next 2 stitches from the left-hand needle; then knit 2 stitches from the cable needle.

Cable 6 back (C6B): Slip the next 3 stitches onto the cable needle and hold at the back of your work. Knit the next 3 stitches from the left-hand needle; then knit 3 stitches from the cable needle.

Cable 6 front (C6F): Slip the next 3 stitches onto the cable needle and hold at the front of your work. Knit the next 3 stitches from the left-hand needle; then knit 3 stitches from the cable needle.

Cable 8 back (C8B): Slip the next 3 stitches onto the cable needle and hold at the back of your work. Knit the next 3 stitches from the left-hand needle; then knit the 3 stitches from the cable needle.

Cable 8 front (C8F): Slip the next 4 stitches onto the cable needle and hold at the front of your work. Knit the next 4 stitches from the left-hand needle; then knit the 4 stitches from the cable needle.

Cross 2 back: Knit into the back of the second stitch on the needle; then knit the first stitch, slipping both stitches off the needle at the same time.

Cross 2 purl: Purl into the front of the second stitch on the needle; then purl the first stitch, slipping both stitches off the needle together.

Cross 2 front: Knit into the front of the second stitch on the needle; then knit the first stitch, slipping both stitches off the needle at the same time.

Cross 6: Slip the next 4 stitches onto the cable needle and hold at the front of your work, knit the next 2 stitches from the left-hand needle; then slip 2 stitches from the cable needle back to the left-hand needle. Pass the cable needle with the 2 remaining stitches to the back of your work, purl the 2 stitches from the left-hand needle; then knit the 2 stitches from the cable needle.

Twist 3 back (T3B): Slip the next stitch onto a cable needle and hold at the back of your work, knit the next 2 stitches from the left-hand needle; then purl the stitch from the cable needle.

Twist 3 front (T3F): Slip the next 2 stitches onto a cable needle and hold at the front of your work, purl the next stitch from the left-hand needle; then knit the 2 stitches from the cable needle.

Useful Information

Abbreviations and Glossary

[ ]	Work instructions within brackets as many times as directed.
( )	Work instructions within parentheses as many times as directed.
*	Repeat instructions following the single asterisk as directed.
**	Repeat instructions between the asterisks as directed.
approx	approximately
beg	begin(ning)
BO	bind off
C4B (C6B, C8B)	cable 4, 6, or 8 back, see "Cable Techniques" on page 93
C4F (C6F, C8F)	cable 4, 6, or 8 front, see "Cable Techniques" on page 93
ch(s)	chain(s)
cm	centimeter(s)
CO	cast on
cont	continue(ing)(s)
dec(s)	decrease(ing)(s)
g	gram(s)
inc(s)	increase(ing)(s)
K	knit
K1f&b	knit into front and back of same stitch—1 stitch increased
K2tog	knit 2 stitches together—1 stitch decreased
kw	knitwise
m	meter(s)
M1	make 1 stitch
M1L	make 1 left, see page 90
M1R	make 1 right, see page 90
mm	millimeter(s)
oz	ounce(s)
P	purl
P2tog	purl 2 stitches together
P3tog	purl 3 stitches together
patt(s)	pattern(s)
pm	place marker
psso	pass slipped stitch over
pw	purlwise
rem	remain(ing)
rep(s)	repeat(s)
rev St st	reverse stockinette stitch
rnd(s)	round(s)
RS	right side
sc	single crochet(s)
sl	slip
sl st(s)	slip stitch(es)
ssk	slip 2 stitches knitwise, 1 at a time, to right needle, then insert left needle from left to right into front loops and knit 2 stitches together—1 stitch decreased
st(s)	stitch(es)
St st(s)	stockinette stitch(es)
T3B	twist 3 sts back, see "Cable Techniques" on page 93
T3F	twist 3 front, see "Cable Techniques" on page 93
tbl	through back loop(s)
tog	together
WS	wrong side
wyib	with yarn in back
wyif	with yarn in front
yb	move yarn to back
yd(s)	yard(s)
yf	move yarn to front
YO(s)	yarn over(s)

Metric Conversions

Yards x .91 = meters
Meters x 1.09 = yards
Grams x .035 = ounces
Ounces x 28.35 = grams

Skill Levels

■□□□ **Beginner:** Projects for first-time knitters using basic knit and purl stitches; minimal shaping.

■■□□ **Easy:** Projects using basic stitches, repetitive stitch patterns, and simple color changes; simple shaping and finishing.

■■■□ **Intermediate:** Projects using a variety of stitches, such as basic cables and lace, simple intarsia, and techniques for double-pointed needles and knitting in the round; midlevel shaping and finishing.

■■■■ **Experienced:** Projects using advanced techniques and stitches, such as short rows, Fair Isle, more intricate intarsia, cables, lace patterns, and numerous color changes.

Standard Yarn-Weight System

Yarn-Weight Symbol and Category Names	1 Super Fine	2 Fine	3 Light	4 Medium	5 Bulky	6 Super Bulky
Types of Yarns in Category	Sock, Fingering, Baby	Sport, Baby	DK, Light worsted	Worsted, Afghan, Aran	Chunky, Craft, Rug	Bulky, Roving
Knit Gauge Ranges in Stockinette Stitch to 4"	27 to 32 sts	23 to 26 sts	21 to 24 sts	16 to 20 sts	12 to 15 sts	6 to 11 sts
Recommended Needle in US Size Range	1 to 3	3 to 5	5 to 7	7 to 9	9 to 11	11 and larger
Recommended Needle in Metric Size Range	2.25 to 3.25 mm	3.25 to 3.75 mm	3.75 to 4.5 mm	4.5 to 5.5 mm	5.5 to 8 mm	8 mm and larger

Stitch Index

About the Author

Doreen L. Marquart taught herself to knit at the age of nine and has been knitting ever since. She didn't become discouraged when people told her they couldn't help her because she is left-handed. Their negative comments just made her more determined to prove them wrong. And prove them wrong she did.

In 1993 Doreen opened Needles 'n Pins Yarn Shoppe at its first location in the front half of a car-and-a-half garage. In 1999, the shop was relocated to its present location . . . a light and spacious 1,200-square-foot custom-designed facility devoted exclusively to the needs of knitters and crocheters. With well over 45,000 skeins of yarn in stock, the shop lures fiberaholics who drive from hours away to "feed their addiction" and to receive help with their knitting and crocheting projects.

Doreen is a master knitter through the Knitting Guild of America as well as a Canadian master knitter and designer. She is also a certified knitting and crocheting instructor through the Yarn Council of America.

Doreen's love of knitting is contagious. She has taught hundreds to knit, from 8 to 80 years of age—even those who had tried to learn elsewhere and given up have proved to themselves that they can indeed knit. She inspires everyone, from beginner to advanced, proving to them that the only thing stopping them from achieving a new goal is themselves. Her motto: If you think you can, you can; if you think you can't, well, you're probably right. Her shop has become a refuge and destination stop for knitters of all levels.

Doreen lives with her husband, Gordon, in Richmond, Wisconsin. They have three grown sons (Michael, Phillip, and Cody), three daughters-in-law (Nicki, Katie, and Melissa), and three granddaughters (Addison, Abbigail, and Nora).

There's More Online
Visit www.needlesnpinsyarnshoppe.com to see other designs by Doreen as well as to learn more about her shop, Needles 'n Pins Yarn Shoppe.